GOING TO PRISON?

Fourth Edition

by Jimmy Tayoun

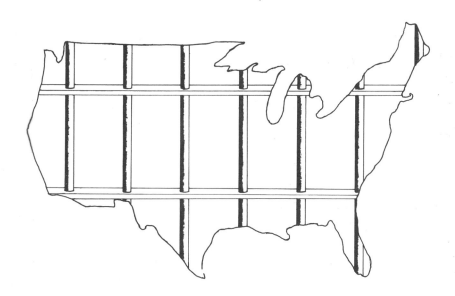

PUBLISHING
COMPANY

PMB 103, PO Box 1305, Brunswick, Maine 04011

Publisher's Cataloging in Publication Data
1. Going to Prison?
2. Tayoun, Jimmy
3. Prisons, Guide to
4. Prisons, Directories
5. Prisons, Visits and Correspondence
6. Prisoners, Handbook for

Title page design by William Bosse

Library of Congress Catalog Card Number 99-073202
ISBN 1-879418-29-0

TABLE OF CONTENTS

Introduction: Welcome to the New World
      Order 5

Part I Pre-Prison Positioning
    Your Probation Officer 6
    Your Timetable 7
    Your Health Needs 10
    Choosing a Prison 12
    Getting To Prison 19

Part 2 Prison Life
    What To Bring 21
    Rules and Regulations 24
    Playing It Safe 35
    Staying Sane 37
    Bait and Switch and the
    Rumor Mill 38
    For Your Family and Friends 38

Epilogue: This Too Shall Pass 39

Appendix A: Glossary 41

Appendix B: Federal Correctional
                Institutions and Camps 45

Appendix C: Community Corrections
                Management Offices
                (Halfway Houses) 73

Appendix D: State Department of
                Corrections 77

About The Author 79

How To Order 80

INTRODUCTION: WELCOME TO THE NEW WORLD ORDER

You have just been sentenced by a federal district judge to a period of incarceration in the federal prison system. And, for what it is worth, each and every week approximately 1,500 people like yourself are being committed by judges around the country to spending various amounts of time in federal prison.

Many more men and women are sentenced to serve time in state and county facilities; if you are among them, most of the information in this manual applies to you too. State prison systems are more subject to variations in administrative policies and operations than that of the federal government. State prisons, therefore, vary in their daily operating rules and regulations not only from state to state, but from county to county. Including federal, state, and county prisons, the incarcerated population in this country continues to challenge the two million mark!

If you are one of the newly sentenced, this booklet is necessary reading for you. It will cushion your fall from the world you know to a "new world order" as a prisoner.

What you will learn as you read through this primer is how to take that initial fall. You will be better able to cope with the shocks of change that assail you during your first days in prison. You will learn how to adapt to the system quickly, and how to serve your time safely and constructively.

We trust you will find the information supportive. It is designed to arm you with a defense through knowledge. It will ease that sharply painful period of initial confusion which works against you when you set foot in the system for the first time. You'll also be aware of why you are being asked certain questions and where your answers can lead you.

You will learn a new vocabulary so that you will know what inmates and officials are talking about when they use such terms as *count-time*, *shot*, *hack*, *call-out*, *change sheet*, *cop out*, *BP9*, *main line*, *short line*, and *shank*.

This book, if it does nothing else, will permit you to position yourself into the best possible role in what is obviously the worst of all scenarios.

PART 1: PRE-PRISON POSITIONING

Your Probation Officer

You will have a probation officer assigned to you the moment you are found guilty or plead guilty. Your probation officer is as important to you as the judge. This is the person who does an investigation of you and writes it up for the judge. His report will say a lot about what happens to you in jail and it will also affect the length of your sentence, as well as whether or not you are a good candidate for the few pre-release programs that currently exist, after you serve a mandatory part of your time.

The PO's background investigation includes interviews with you, your family and friends. He comes to your home and/or your business and he checks up on every bit of information you give him. By the time he writes his report, he will know what you are really worth financially, what your family and friends really think about you, and will have discovered if you have any other skeletons in the closet.

He will listen to all as though he were a sympathetic old friend. He could be. But he could also be your biggest headache! So you say nothing to him that cannot be supported in writing or by the testimony of others.

His finished report is given to the judge. It officially becomes the PSI or the Pre-Sentence Investigation packet that follows you everywhere.

How the probation officer comes away from the interviews with your family and you — and they are usually conducted separately — will have an influence on what he recommends to the judge, either to go the lowest or push to the highest in a particular sentence range.

You do get a copy of his Pre-Sentence Investigation. Your copy is the same as the one the judge receives, but it does not include probation officer recommendations. You must go over that report with a fine-tooth comb. If there is anything in it that does not ring true for you and your attorney, immediately call it to the probation officer's attention. He will rectify the error, and the correction could be important — for example, some violation for which you are still being charged, but was dropped as part of the plea-bargain agreement. Your probation officer is neither a trained accountant nor tax specialist. He relies on dollar figures charged against you. If you question these figures, document your reasons and hand your explanation to your probation officer as soon as possible.

Unless your mind has been racing ahead to the time you plan to plead guilty, odds are you would not have worried about a booklet like this. And the odds are you will have had your initial interview in which you spent an hour or two filling out forms and answering questions.

But now you have this guide and you have discovered your responses were not as complete as they could have been when the probation officer first interviewed you. After all, it is common for people under stress to forget a lot of things, consider them to be irrelevant, even though later they could have a very relevant role in how they spend prison time. You may not, for instance, remember that you have a bad back that will not permit you to jump up to and down from a top bunk. So if you go to the doctor who listens to your complaints and documents them, you can now take that back to the PO for inclusion in his report.

The PSI is in your file at the prison when you get there. It is reviewed frequently by the prison counselors, the education people, the administrators and the members of the team that watch and judge and control your movement throughout your tenure at the institution. They also determine whether or not you will be considered for a furlough or community custody so that, in case of an emergency, your family can pick you up and bring you back, rather than a marshal or custodial officer escorting you to your home in handcuffs.

One important fact to remember about the PSI is that everyone identified in it as a family member is approved for visiting almost without delay. We will discuss visiting privileges in detail further on. But, for now, note that if you have an adopted child or are a guardian for someone, inform the probation officer. Tell him you need these persons listed as members of the immediate family. List also sons- and daughters-in-law as immediate members. Doing so at this time will enable them to visit you quickly.

Your Timetable

Sentencing
In your Pre-Sentencing Investigation, the Probation Officer has figured out how many points you earned through your real or alleged transgressions against the law. Each charge to which you plead guilty has a number of points assigned to it. The judge knows by the number of points

what latitude he has in passing sentence. He knows the minimum and the maximum amount of time he can hand out. For a judge to drop a sentence below the minimum or "below the guidelines," he risks a great deal of criticism and must do a lot of justifying, usually in briefs that require significant research and writing. Judges are opposed to their sentencing judgments being restricted. Amendments permitting more discretion have since begun filtering in.

A bit of the Sentencing Table is reproduced here, so you can get a pretty good idea of how the judge will figure your time. Your PSI report will have a page that indicates the category, from I through VI, in which you are placed and the Level of the crime or crimes to which you pled guilty or have been adjudged guilty. If, for example, your PSI indicates you to be at Offense Category I and your crime at Level 10, the Judge will sentence you to a minimum of 6 months or a maximum of 12. Although the table is changed from time to time, recent amendments affect only the degree to which the judge may depart from these guidelines, either to increase or decrease the sentencing time.

If you are plea bargaining, your lawyer and you need to do some hard bargaining in the "Level" area. As you can see, the lower the level, the shorter the prison term. Alternative sentences, such as house arrest or boot camp (see Glossary), are also worth bargaining for if you qualify.

You will have a brief period of time between the day you are found guilty or plead guilty and the day when you report back to the judge for sentencing. Sometimes your lawyer can have this time interval extended. In cases where a guilty plea has been entered, sparing the U.S. Attorney's Office a costly trial, the judge will more than likely agree not only to this request, but also to an even longer period between the time he sentences you and the time you have to report to prison.

It is in this brief time span that you can lobby the judge, through your attorney, to request that he assign you, in his sentencing order, to the prison that will best suit your needs and your family's. Especially do not hesitate to make this request if you are a nonviolent first-time offender.

Your attorney transmits your request to the judge either by phone or in writing. He will base the request on family or health needs. He must never suggest that you might want to be at a specific institution because it would be easier to continue running your business from there, or because you'd like to spend your time in a warm, sunny clime.

SENTENCING TABLE*
Criminal History Category

Offense Level	I (0-1)	II (2-3)	III (4-6)	IV (7-9)	V (10-12)	VI (13+)
1	0-6	0-6	0-6	0-6	0-6	0-6
2	0-6	0-6	0-6	0-6	0-6	1-7
3	0 6	0-6	0-6	0-6	2-8	3-9
4	0-6	06	0-6	2-8	4-10	6 12
5	0-6	0 6	1-7	4-10	6-12	9-15
6	0-6	1-7	2-8	6 12	9-15	12-18
7	1-7	2-8	4-10	8-14	12-18	15-21
8	2-8	4-10	6 12	1-16	15-21	18-24
9	4-10	6-12	8-14	12-18	18-24	21-27
10	6-12	8-14	10-16	15-21	21-27	24-30
11	8-14	10-16	12-18	18-24	24-30	27-33
12	10-16	12-18	15-21	21-27	27-33	30-37
13	12-18	15-21	18-24	24-30	30-37	33-41
14	15-21	18-24	21-27	27-33	33-41	37-46
15	18-24	21-27	24-30	30-37	37-46	41-51
16	21-27	24-30	27-33	33-41	41-51	46-57
17	24-30	27-33	30-37	37-46	46-57	51-63
18	27-33	30-37	33-41	41-51	51-63	57-71
19	30-37	33-41	37-46	46-57	57-71	63-78

U.S.C. Annotated Title 18, Crimes and Criminal Procedures, #4121 to End, 1996

The government brings charges against you, which they must prove. If they prove them or you plead to them, then they become crimes, such as embezzlement, fraud, murder, conspiracy, etc. Each crime—or "offense" —has affixed to it a number of points. Your category is I if you have never been found guilty before and II if you have been found guilty in the past. If you have been found guilty of more than one offense, your probation officer will give you the point level for each offense. That total is your offense level, and under the category that fits is where you will find the sentence that you can expect from the judge, a minimum to a maximum.

Reducing Your Sentence

Once you're in, you want to know when you're getting out. When you learn that, you'll want to figure out what you need to do to get out earlier.

You will receive a "print out" of your sentencing history which includes your maximum time (known by inmates as "to the door") and your GCT (good credit time). Before 1987, GCT had been as much as 104 days per year, only to be reduced after that year to 54 days; it may well change again while you are in prison. Sad to say, but true, once you become the property of the Bureau of Prisons you are controlled by their policies as to early release, unless you have submitted a sentencing appeal or have asked for a new trial, either of which may result in a downward revision of your sentence.

Technically, however, you can get an earlier release ! It comes about toward the end of your term. If you have earned good credit time and have not gotten involved in any disciplinary problems, you could look forward to half way house time for up to 10% of your time served. No matter how long your sentence, the maximum amount of time afforded by this policy for half way houses is six months.

Prison overcrowding pressures may dictate how liberal each institution gets in its policies; a warden's attitude is also reflected in their application. One institution may think a half way house time of two to four months is generous enough, while another may automatically confer six monthers on their departing inmates.

There are programs designed to cut sentences by a minimum of a year. Ask and you shall receive! The Bureau of Prisons may have a program in which you could fit at the end of which your reward is a reduction in the time you need to serve. One, seemingly successful and quite sought after by inmates, involves spending a year in intensive physical "army style" basic training coupled with a heavy dose of group therapy.

Serious illness does not factor as a way of getting out of prison earlier. Whatever the illness, the prison system has accredited medical facilities to address it. Forget your need for an organ transplant. No matter how serious your need, it won't be possible for you to undertake one until you are back home.

When you hear an inmate brag he's "going to the door," know that is his way of making himself feel good, despite the fact he did his time the wrong and hard way, bringing down enough incident reports upon himself to lose his GCT. Congratulate him. Odds are he really thinks he beat the system-he did it his way.

Your Health Needs

Y ou also need the pre-sentencing time to take care of the "physical you"-the one with the teeth that need cleaning and fixing, the one with the eyes that need new glasses, the one with the aching back, the one that has to take pills or insulin every day.

So get to your favorite dentist and make sure he checks your teeth thoroughly and repairs whatever his x-rays tell him need repairing. You don't have time for cosmetic surgery. Eliminate the fancy work, and get to the fundamentals. Tell the dentist you want these repairs to last the length of your duration in prison. Make sure that any borderline teeth, that could hint at cavities, get pre-emptive surgery — and "Please, Doc, do it all in three days!"

If you wear glasses, make sure your ophthalmologist gives you an up-to-date prescription, take it to the optician and get yourself two pairs of glasses — the one you wear and the extra to take with you. Again, stick to fundamentals, nothing fancy schmantzy. Try to get frames with as few screws in them as possible. Once you lose a screw in prison, it may be gone for the duration — your glasses will have to be held together with masking tape. The commissaries of some institutions sell replacement kits. If you need reading glasses, carry them in with you on a halter string around your neck, so you look "professorial." Pack the second in with the other material you take with you to prison.

Orthotics or other foot inner soles should be brought with you since most prison footwear is not designed with this need in mind.

If you know you are not the outdoors type or that you do not have the agility to hop up to a top bunk or to jump down from one — it is about five feet above the ground — or that you cannot lift heavy objects or that you suffer from allergies or that you are a two-pillow sleeper, then rush off to your favorite physician. Tell him what is about to happen to you, and ask if he can justify all those "cannots" and "needs" and to do so by putting them in writing. If you have far more serious ailments and require specific medications daily, by all means, you need documentation and plenty of supplies to take with you. This is necessary to make sure that, until the prison doctors confirm what you and your doctor are telling them, you have enough medicine on hand for two weeks. Now take the doctor's reports to the probation officer. You want to make sure he includes this information in his PSI.

Choosing a Prison

Sometimes you have no choice — but most times you do! You do not when you are considered a maximum-security type — an organized crime leader, a member of a drug cartel, a chronic offender with a previous criminal history, or someone involved in situations which included weapons.

The Federal Penal system over the years has learned that not all criminals are cut from the same cloth; its prisons have been tailored to fit the type of felon they are to house.

The Federal system groups and designs its prisons by security levels. Its governing board, the people who run the system, and its various district offices or regions are known as the Bureau of Prisons. The BOP decides if a prison should be for males or females and ranks prisons by security level as minimum, low, medium, high, or administrative. Administrative facilities are usually those with special functions such as providing care for medical and mental patients who are criminals. According to the BOP Facilities Guide, the ranking is based on "the evaluation of seven security features — the presence of external patrols, gun towers, security barriers, detection devices, type of housing, internal security features, and the inmate-to-correctional-officer ratio."

Some of the Federal Prisons around this country look like church edifices. Others remind you of monasteries or state capitols or resort hotels. Some of the older ones look like throwbacks to medieval castles, but those built in the last two decades look pretty much alike. The BOP also contracts out for the operation of about 300 halfway houses (also known as community corrections centers) for offenders who are winding down in their time, that is, are within 30 to 180 days of their maximum release date.

Whatever they look like, BOP facilities are all run with the mission of "maintaining safe, secure, and humane correctional institutions and implementing correctional programs that strive for a balance between punishment, deterrence, incapacitation, and rehabilitation." (BOP Facilities Report).

Into which hole your peg fits depends on how you are evaluated by the BOP custody classification system. There are four custody levels to which you may be assigned: **Out Custody** (including Community

Custody and Minimum Security Camps) and **In Custody** (including Low, Medium and Maximum Security facilities). Your probation officer can make available to you a print-out that describes the physical plant, location, programs and some of the policies of the prison to which you wish to be sent, if possible, or to which you have already been "designated."

Out Custody: Community Custody

This means you are allowed to leave the prison facility without an escort for family emergencies or a furlough of a day or two and may actually be allowed to go into the nearest town on errands for the prison. It may also mean you are assigned to a halfway house, usually located in or close to your city.

Since you have been deprived of the best possible custody level — which is not to have to go to jail in the first place — your second best is to attempt to have part of your sentence committed to a half-way house stay. These stays are usually no more than six months in length, but would be a boon to you at the downside of your term. Half-way houses are located in or near big cities or metropolitan areas. They are extensions of the prison, but are not built as such. Usually they are found in converted old loft buildings on the fringes of the main part of town. You are required to sleep in them every night, return by a certain hour, and report to work on time every morning. Some half-way houses permit you to visit your family between the hours when work ends and the time you must return. Most allow weekend visits home once you begin to work at a paying job.

Out Custody: Minimum Security Camps

Out-Custody means assignment to a camp or a minimum security facility where there are no fences or gates and where you are literally outside the fence or wall. Most first-time offenders, unless they are big time in whatever it was they were doing, will be given the Out-Custody designations. This means they go to a Federal Prison Camp.

These facilities have no perimeter fences, no guarded gates, no security towers, no roving guards with guns, and no bars in evidence anywhere. But make no mistake — they are prisons!

Prior to 1987 when a change in sentencing guidelines limited the license of judges to sentence as they saw fit, the average term of a camper was about two years. Today, with judges constrained to predetermined sentence lengths, it is not unusual to find campers with as much as eight years to serve, sentence terms that would normally have put them in medium security prisons.

Long-termers are finding their way into the camp system because they meet all the requirements of a camp inmate —first-time non-weapon offense, a good community background, solid middle-class family, and generally responsible behavior. Judges not only recommend such persons to camps but also recommend them to low-security prisons as well. Camps are not restricted to first-time offenders only. They are also for well-behaved inmates, nearing the end of long imprisonments, transferred from higher security institutions.

Campers have more freedom than their contemporaries in the higher security institutions. Campers can literally disappear into their cubicles, to the TV room, to play cards, to the ball field, to the gym and weight rooms, or to just hang out without "checking in with a custodial officer to have a slip signed indicating he has been approved to go to another part of the institution."

Camps physically have a campus look to them. The inmate housing is dormitory style for the most part. The buildings dedicated to housing normally have four dormitories or "ranges" within them. Each dormitory is subdivided into small cubicles with enough space for a double bunk, some minimal furniture and storage space, and usually one chair.

The housing units also have within them two recreational rooms dedicated to television viewing, one of which is usually referred to as sports TV and the other general programming. The main administration building is designed to include a community mess hall; a general library with a law library section; an infirmary for medical, dental and optometry services; possibly a gym or — at the very least — an indoor exercise area devoted to weight lifting; administrative offices; a conference room; a laundry room; arts and crafts space; sometimes a chapel; and a large visiting room which also doubles on occasion for a meeting room or an assembly hall. The remainder of the campus is given over to basketball courts, a ball field, a racquet court and a walking path along the entire perimeter.

Campers quickly learn where on the grounds they may walk and where they may not, when they can do what they wish to and when they must be back in their cubes or at work. To remain campers, they learn to

14

be model minimum-security types who can be trusted "outside of the fence." What prevents camp inmates from misbehaving is the knowledge that they can easily be transferred to any Federal Correctional Institution and then assigned a more restrictive designation as a low-security or medium-security inmate, if they persist in not following instructions. The record against them builds up with what are called *shots* — incident reports of prohibited actions which, after investigation, are rated according to severity. A low shot means extra hours of work; a severe one means off to the segregation cell at the FCI or at a local county jail and farewell to camps until the end of the inmate's term.

In-Custody: Low and Medium Security

In-Custody puts you into an institution that has fencing, usually doubled-up barbed-wire rolls three to six rolls high, guarded entrances, and a constant roving patrol. The higher the security rating of a prison, the less freedom of movement you may expect. Prisoners are more closely monitored in prisons housing low-level and medium-security inmates than in Camps.

You are placed into these facilities for a variety or combination of reasons including type of crime, length of sentence, the number of co-defendants, if and how violence was used, or if you are a repeat offender.

Another way is for you to make yourself a "problem" if assigned to a Camp. Enough infractions of the rules can lead you to being booked into one of these facilities and taken there after a stint of "diesel therapy" (see Glossary).

Movements must be constantly restricted, timed, and totally monitored in such facilities. Here you learn what the term "controlled movement" means. You cannot move from one place to another until the hour mark and must complete your movement within ten minutes after the hour mark.

You also cannot move around at these times unless you have a pass issued you by the Custodial Officer in charge of where you are at the moment, which you must hand over to the officer in charge of the area where you plan to go.

In-Custody: Maximum Security

Another name for maximum security prisons is penitentiary. These are walled-in facilities. Once inside the wall you know the difference. The world always looks darker and gloomier than it really is because of the high surrounding walls of stone that dominate your entire life, and the watchtowers strategically located on top or adjacent to them from which guards scan every movement, day or night.

Penitentiaries house two types of population: the general population and the "lock-down" population.

Penitentiary living is similar in most respects to lower level FCIs, but your work assignments are less varied. It is either food service or landscaping, the latter usually a form of keeping the grounds free of litter and cigarette butts.

Inmates are rougher and tougher and yet more respectful of each other's space. But when space is violated, it can be painful in more ways than one. Inmates also have a tendency to gather in clans for obvious reasons, and here you are able to identify their membership easily. Among the groups found in penitentiaries are the Muslim Brotherhood, the Aryan Brotherhood, Bikers, Chicanos (Puerto Ricans), and the Marieletos (Cuban exiles via Port Mariel).

Inmates in penitentiaries try to keep busy the full day, working overtime if allowed, by signing on to work at UNICOR (Prison Industries factory) if one is available, and involving themselves heavily in arts and crafts.

Life in a penitentiary is very trying if you are in the lock-down population. (These are usually inmates with an extremely violent history, or who have created trouble at other prisons, are higher escape risks, or belong to major organized crime families or drug cabals.) You are literally locked down 23 hours of the day. You do not work. When you request a shower and it is permitted, you are escorted from your cell to a shower room in cuffs and shackles. There you turn in your dirty clothes and are given clean ones after showering. Exercise is permitted for an hour a day, the hour of your choosing. You may not come back to your cell, should you desire, before the hour is up. Exercise is mostly a solitary affair, though on some weekends several others in nearby cells may, along with you, be allowed into the small exercise yard together to play a game of basketball.

Here, as everywhere, phone calls are terminated after 15 minutes. The phone is handed to you through your cell door food slot after the guard dials the number for you. Commissary slips are taken from you

16

once a week and a paper bag is brought back to you with your requests. The bottom line here is you live out your sentence in a small cell around 5 by 7 feet with a bolted down cot, a john, a sink, and a small table with a hinged chair as your furnishings.

Chow time is handled differently in penitentiaries for the general population. While the lock-downs eat in their cells, the general population is allowed to enter the food service one cell block at a time. You come in one way, go out another, have a limited time to eat, and together return to your duties or your cells. All this is done to prevent confrontations in the dining room and to keep the numbers eating at one time to a controllable force.

Making Your Choice

You have a large selection of prisons to choose from these days. At least five new federal prisons, the majority of them with Satellite Camps, are opening each year with still more planned. The 1987 changing of the sentence guidelines has contributed to that phenomenon. More people getting longer terms means fewer people being released which, in turn, means the need for more prisons. It also means prison overcrowding.

In this book you will see prisons listed with their population capacity. Those numbers are more truthful if you double them. The population capacity merely indicates how many bunks can fit into the place. It does not indicate the fact that you can pile one bunk four feet above another and house two inmates in the same cube, a common practice all over the Federal Prison System.

In Appendix B is a list of brief descriptions of most of the prisons now on line in the Federal Prison system — their capacity, location, and other nuggets of information you may want to take into consideration before you make your choices. In the hope that the judge will send you to one of your choices, you should suggest three, in order of priority. Suggesting more than three is not a good idea. It may lead the judge to feel that your requests are being made without sound, rational motivation. Listed are maximum, medium, low-level, and minimum security facilities. You can lobby only for low-level and minimum security placement.

What are rational reasons for preferring one prison over another? Some prisons are simply more "inviting" than others, having the reputation of being Fed Meds (after the vacation clubs in the Caribbean). But you may want to weigh comfort against distance. One prison could be within an hour to two hours drive from your home, while those offering better climate, more walking space, more recreation facilities, or superior educational programs may require too much money and time from family members who want to visit you as often as you would like to have them visit.

Here are a couple more tips to use as a guide. (1) Look for a camp that stands by itself, and is not a satellite. If adjacent to an FCI, the camp plays second fiddle to the needs of the bigger sister with regard to the staff, supplies, requests, and recreational facilities. The administrators of these camps lean a bit more in favor of the campers if they do not have an FCI warden and staff looking down at them from the bigger facility down the street. When that is the case, there is a tendency to increase regimentation unnecessarily in the satellite camp. As a result, camp officials are slow at building rapport with the inmates. Some poor souls, who resent being "pushed around," take it out on themselves by refusing to take advantage of programs offered that are designed to help them. (2) Look for a camp located adjacent to or on an existing military base. Inmates are often used as back-up to do the drudgery work — the BOP calls this "providing basic services" — for the base. Food at such facilities is usually better, and you get to work and interact for part of the day with people who are not employees of the prison system. Besides, because the facilities are spread out over more ground, there are more opportunities for exercise. Remember, unless you have two left feet and they hurt all the time, walking is one of the most important forms of recreation available to you.

Appendix B will tell you where the prisons are, how to get to them, and what they "offer."

Getting to Prison

There is no such thing as a free ride! Some people never learn that basic fact of life. So when they are asked if they are going to report to the prison themselves, which means paying their own way, they elect to let the federal marshals take them. An unwise decision!

The consequence of choosing to let the government pay for the transportation is this: the judge will either order you to be taken away at once or — at best — he may give you a time to report to the marshal's office in the District Court House where you found yourself on trial.

Whatever the case, the moment you report to the marshal, you get clamped into a cell where you wait for the bus that will take you and other prisoners to jail, a trip known as the "diesel tour." To get to your camp or FCI, the bus will probably stop at several prisons en route, picking up prisoners being transferred to your prison or another one on the circuit and dropping some off. Throughout this ride, you are handcuffed in such a way that you are lucky to be able to hold the sandwich or drink the beverage they give you during the day.

Odds are you will be disgorged at another prison, which of necessity must be of a high security level, and put into its holding area — a very crowded huge pen-type room with insufficient toilets — or into a small segregation cell. Here you may remain for anywhere from a day to several months waiting for the bus to return and take you to your destination.

That's why those who self-surrender and pay their own way are the wiser. What they spend in money to rent a car, or to put gasoline into a friend's tank, or to host the family going up with them is more than compensated by the amount of discomfort saved.

Now that you have told the judge you would prefer to report directly to your assigned prison and he gives you a reporting date, you should arrange to get there by 2 p.m. If you arrive later, the Receiving and Dismissal people are annoyed because it will delay their quitting time. It means that many of the things that you can have done that day, like having your clothes tailored to fit, will be delayed until the next day or next week. Arriving soon after noon means the R & D staff have just returned from lunch and have some energy to do a decent job in rushing you through the "humbling" process of being stripped, fingerprinted and photographed. Hopefully, you will be given bus pants, blue bus shoes, and a coat (if it is cold), without having to stand in the hallway for a while before they call you back for the next step.

Go with the flow! You might find yourself cold, hungry, or thirsty during this short period. You may also feel abandoned when you trade your clothing for prison garb, which may range from dull brown and shabby greens to embarrassing bright orange.

One more benefit of arriving by yourself is that prison officials are more willing to allow you to bring in some of your personal belongings if they do not have to handle an additional half dozen people who came off the bus with you.

PART 2: PRISON LIFE

What To Bring

In reality, you do not have to take anything but the clothes you are wearing. Leave at home keys, wallet, pens and pencils, credit cards — you won't need them. Do know that your basic needs will be provided you! Suggestion: wear a plain sweat suit — odds are they may let you keep it. In any event, bring a good amount of cash if you can. You'll see why as you read on.

If you let the marshal's office take you, the personal luggage you brought may not catch up with you for several weeks after you've arrived at your final destination. But if you are self-surrendering, what you bring in, you will be able to take to your cubicle with you. You will sleep this first night with some of your familiar clothes and toiletries.

After you have said good-bye to your family and friends or whoever accompanied you, one of the Receiving and Dismissal people will be alerted to your presence as you approach the reception room near the front of the main door. He or she will take you into the R & D office. A male guard (for male prisoners) will then escort you to a room where there are lots of identical type garments and shoes. He will ask you to strip, search all your clothes and ask — or guess — your shirt size and length of pants. He will give you a set of bus pants, the kind with the rubber waist band that fits many sizes, or plain khaki pants and a shirt, stockings and a pair of bus sneakers. Women are given full skirts, blouses, and the basic bras and panties. One prison, Alderson, WV, permits women prisoners to wear their own clothing. Then the guard will send you back out to get fingerprinted and photographed. Soon you will be handed your own personal commissary card, which serves as a credit card and i.d. card. How you use this card will be explained in the next section under "Commissary."

In the meantime, you are negotiating with one of the R & D people about the material you brought in. What can you keep with you? About some items, they will arbitrarily say "no" to you while permitting another inmate to bring in the identical items. There is no rationale behind this, so get used to it: you are now a prisoner of Uncle Sam!

Besides signing your name to a lot of forms, you will be given a net woven laundry bag (looking like fish net so that the contents can be easily seen whenever you carry it around) and told to stuff into it: 3 sets of pants, 3 shirts, 6 undershirts, 6 underpants, 6 pairs of white sweat stockings, 1 khaki jacket, 2 sheets, 1 pillow and pillow case, and 2 blankets. You are also issued a pair of boots which you carry. You are instructed to take the clothing to the laundry where inmates will measure and cut and hem the trousers to fit. Women prisoners receive the same number of items, but sometimes colors other than khaki are used.

Know that some of the forms you will be asked to sign waive your rights away. They include agreeing to having your telephone calls monitored, not to make business calls, and to having your mail opened, as well as having them deposit your funds into a general account, distributing your share to you as you need it.

Then your camp counselor or the custodial officer on duty will escort you to one of the housing units. He will take you into his little office, lecture you about what is expected of you, and have the unit orderly bring you your personal toiletries. These include one or two bars of soap, a couple of small tubes of toothpaste, a soft tooth brush, some cheap plastic razors, a small plastic comb, a lined writing pad, a pencil, and some envelopes.

That is your welcome home package.

On the following day, it' s a good idea to ask the custodial officer for a couple more razors, some more soap, and later for tooth paste. After a while you will learn where it is stored, check the door until you find it open, and help yourself. But never take too much since your lockers do get checked.

But we' re getting ahead of our story. Let' s return to the R & D office where you are looking over your belongings with the office clerk who is signing you in. The items listed below are usually acceptable at most prisons, whether FCIs or camps. Each institution has its own idiosyncrasies, permitting items to come in that other institutions are refusing. The main problem prisons have is insufficient space, and the space you are allotted reflects this shortage. More institutions are limiting what you can bring to a religious medal, a wedding band, eye glasses, and needed braces. Your personal storage space is limited and there is just no other place available to you during these early days.

If you're lucky, you'll be allowed to keep with you...

1 address book, 2 religious books, 5 hardcover books and 5 softcover books

up to 3 cubic feet of your personal legal materials — your PSI report, letters from the lawyer, indictment papers, plea agreements, your case file

2 baseball style caps (plain and not Navy blue)

30 packs of cigarettes

1 plastic container (the large kind that you get at McDonalds for soda, but more durable)

2 eyeglass cases

2 sets of eyeglasses

30 photos (this number varies down to 10)

1 religious medal on a chain valued under $100

1 wedding ring, plain band

1 watch, value under $100 (sometimes)

2 pairs of sneaks or walking shoes

1 pair of regular dress shoes

1 set of shower slippers

5 pairs of athletic socks

2 handball exercise gloves

1 headband

2 wrist braces and 2 ankle braces

3 jogging and/or sweat suits, preferably plain, definitely without logos

1 weight-lifter belt

2 athletic supporters

1 mouthpiece

2 thigh braces

2 gym shorts

6 tee shirts

4 sets of underwear

3 pair of work socks.

— and that is it.

They will not allow you to bring in a Walkman type radio and head phone or some other items that would have contributed nicely to your stay, like an electric razor. You can shave with better razors than those issued by purchasing them from the commissary.

After this ritual, you place what is not approved into a cardboard carton, possibly along with the clothes you wore when you arrived. You address the carton, and they send it off to your family. At this moment you understand that there was once a time when you came into this world naked, and now you have been born again, made naked, and brought re-clothed to this new world order — where everyone gives orders and you take them.

Rules and Regulations

Every institution gives you an "Admissions and Orientation Inmate Handbook," a set of mimeographed pages stapled at one corner — your bible. It tells all there is to know about the institution as far as you are concerned. It tells you what is open and at what time of the day. The information is vital, but you receive it after you get in and not before, when you could have used it to answer questions that normally come to mind. This section is intended to answer those questions.

Each prison handbook starts off with a statement of its mission and by reminding inmates to "maintain your living area in a satisfactory manner and maintain your personal appearance and hygiene in an accepted manner." The remainder of the booklet covers the following information:

Clothing Exchange
Bed linens can be exchanged almost any morning, blankets on specific days. This depends on where you are. Torn or unserviceable clothing can be exchanged on assigned days. In camps, washing and drying your clothes is up to you. Washers, dryers, and soap are available in every housing building. In higher level institutions, you hand in your bundle at prescribed times and pick it up when told it will be ready.

Commissary
The commissary makes money for the institution. The first words you read in your booklet under this heading are "It is a privilege — not a right — for inmates to participate in the commissary program. The warden, or his representative, may deny or limit that privilege at any time."

Commissary funds come from a trust fund account set up for you in your name with money that you brought in, with what has been sent to you from outside sources, and with the pay you earn as a worker either with UNICOR or with the institution. Every time money comes in to you from the outside, you will receive a receipt. If money from the outside comes in a form other than in cash, postal money orders, or Western Union money orders, it will be as long as 15 days before the money is posted to your account.

Every commissary issues an order form, which lists a whole host of things — tobacco to toiletries, candies to food and fruit.

The food comes in the form of pop-open cans, soup mixes, and packages of candies, nuts, and even ice cream. A special section lists a host of various items ranging from radios to shoe laces to shoe polish to weight-lifting gloves and finally sneakers and gym clothes.

The commissary trust-fund account is computerized, the bar codes on the back of your card registering how much money is in your account. What you order is automatically subtracted from the account as each item is passed over a scanner. Commissary hours are short, and you are limited as to how much you can spend each month, the usual maximum being $150. The amount you don't spend for the month is not carried over to the next.

Contraband

This means anything not issued to you by the staff, or purchased by you from the commissary, or allowed in with you by R & D. And it also applies to containers from which the original contents have been removed and are now used by you to store other items. Anything identified as contraband is confiscated.

Count Times

A top priority for running a prison is knowing that your charges have not flown the coop, that they are still around. They count you at midnight, 2:30 a.m., 5:00 a.m., 4:15 p.m. and 9 p.m. The 4:15 p.m. count is a stand-up count, which means that you must be standing and quiet in front of your cell or cube entrance, so that the two officers who do the count can see you. These count times occur every day, year round. On weekends, a 10:00 a.m. count is added, since you did not have to report to work and you could have easily left the corral to do a little gallivanting right after the 5:00 a.m. count, not getting back until 4:15 p.m. The 10 a.m. weekend and holiday count is designed to put a crimp in such plans.

Disciplinary procedures

Should you be cited by the staff and given an incident report and then have lodged against you a "shot," there are ways to appeal it. The appeal procedures will be listed in your bulletin in detail. It will also list the "prohibited acts and disciplinary severity scale." This scale takes the form of charts graded into four "codes" — 100 code (for example, drug use or disruption of prison security), 200 code (fighting, engaging in sexual acts or work stoppage), 300 code (insolence or lying to staff member, violating furlough), 400 code (malingering, possession of another's property, inappropriate conduct with a visitor), with 100 as the severest in disciplinary sanctions. Sanctions include severe penalties such as transfer, segregation and loss of job to lesser ones such as reprimand and extra duty. Also listed in your bulletin are your rights and responsibilities as an inmate.

Education

All Bureau of Prison facilities now require that you graduate from their control with at least a high school diploma. So if you don't have one, you may be required to get one before you qualify for an early release program for which you might otherwise be eligible. Courses that permit inmates to work toward college degrees are offered in most institutions. And if your language is other than English, you will have to take an English as a Second Language course to gain proficiency. Some vocational training exists at camps, but the better programs are found at FCIs.

Food

Don't expect home cooking and do get ready for a lot of starchy foods — plenty of pasta and rice and potatoes. Breakfast is early, usually at 6 a.m. with service ending an hour later. On weekends, only two meals are served — brunch after the 10:00 a.m. count and dinner after the 4:15 p.m. count.

The "short line" is for on-duty food service workers and other inmates who must be on duty before the main line serving time. Short-line food is decidedly better than what is served on the main line. The cooks always take good care of themselves, and the cadre want their workers contented. "Common fare" is provided for those on restricted and religious diets, including kosher diets, but you must arrange this with the help of the chaplain. The dress code is enforced for different meals, so check your specific institution's rules.

Infirmary

Sick calls are scheduled almost every day with hours listed when you can ask for headache or fever pills or antihistamines, for medical services, and for scheduling dental and other examinations. All inmates get a once over, including a blood test and a couple of x-rays, when they arrive.

Only when you can prove to the physician's assistants who serve you that they are not up to handling your illness, and then only after the resident physician agrees that you need it, is consultation permitted by an orthopedist or a surgeon or a dermatologist, ophthalmologist, cardiologist, etc. And if you need an operation, you will probably be transferred to one of several facility prisons run by the BOP.

Normally you will be tested for an HIV status prior to your release Make sure you begin badgering the infirmary for the blood test at least two months before your projected release date. Not getting the test past you by then could result in a delay of your release unless you are "maxing out". Otherwise you will be periodically tested for AIDS if you display clinic signs of HIV infection, or have noticeable predatory or promiscuous behavior. The majority of infected inmates remain in the general population if their physical condition and their behavior permits.

If you want to go the mental route, hoping you'll get your time reduced, you open a pandora's box for yourself. So don't play games!

Law library

Yes, every institution has a law library to which every inmate normally heads to discover some glitch in the law that his lawyer has overlooked, or some opportunity for an appeal based on a recent ruling on a case similar to his. The law library is supervised by the Education Department which also provides typewriters, legal stationery, carbon paper, and sometimes a copier for inmates to use in preparing legal materials for court. You pay for photocopies, when you need them, with your commissary card.

Mail

All mail (other than special mail) coming in to you from the real world is opened and inspected. If the envelopes include anything else but paper — for example stamps or medals — such items are removed and confiscated and sometimes returned to the sender. When this occurs, you receive a copy of the notation that accompanies the item being returned.

Outgoing mail is uncensored, but the upper left hand corner of the envelope must bear your name, registration number, unit number, and the institution address, or it will not be mailed.

"Special" mail — mail from attorneys, politicians, courts, military officials — does not get opened except in your presence by your counselor, who hands it to you to demonstrate that the letter has not been read by anyone from the prison administration. "Special mail" will get opened earlier unless it has printed or typed on the face of the envelope: SPECIAL MAIL — TO BE OPENED IN PRESENCE OF INMATE ONLY. If an attorney is a member of a firm, his name must appear as part of the return address of the firm in the top left corner.

As for packages, you don't get any — unless you make proper arrangements in advance. It works like this. To obtain, for example, a specific item of clothing, you first have to obtain approval to request it from the infirmary physician or the chaplain or your unit manager. If the item you request is approved, you are given to forward to the sender a special form which is to be included in the package. When the package arrives, it is opened and inspected. If the authorization slip is packed with it, you get the article of clothing. Otherwise, it goes back.

You may receive as many as five softcover books at any one time from anyone. But the word *books* must appear on the outside of the package. You may receive hardback books only if they are mailed from a book store or a publisher. Books can be turned back, especially magazines, if the warden feels they are "detrimental to the security, good order or discipline of the institution, and promote criminal activity" (like how to make bombs or ammunition from blanket lint, for example).

You may subscribe to as many magazines and newspapers as you want, provided you have the money to have them delivered. Forms are provided for a transfer of funds for that purpose. It's easier all around if family or friends pre-pay the subscription. Note that the magazines usually arrive about the same time you would have gotten them at home, while the newspapers are always two to four days late.

Off Limits
Unless you are performing authorized work on a work detail or on a call out, you will discover that nearly all areas in FCI's or camps are off-limits. You are permitted only in your designated housing area (the building in which you live), the dining room, the education complex, the chapel and

in designated inside and outside recreation areas. You are restricted to the sidewalks. You are not permitted to walk on any unpaved area with the exception of the recreation yard or unless authorized to do so by a staff member.

Radios

Personal radios are allowed if they are small and can only be used with ear phones. Institutions make such radios available for purchase through the commissary. You will not be permitted to bring a radio in, no matter how good or how cheap. Also the institutions are emphatically opposed to tape recorders or players.

Radio playing can be a nuisance when you are trying to sleep. The fact that the radio can be played only through ear phones reduces that probability, but be warned that some inmates have learned how to amplify the sound that comes from their ear phones. You will moan while you marvel at their ingenuity.

Recreation

The recreation department handles indoor and outdoor recreational activities, monitors them, and considers its inside recreation sites as no-smoking areas. Most institutions have recreation areas that include a hobby craft center, a weight room, a music room, and a game room, some with one or two pocket billiard tables. Other small table games include fooze ball and bumper pool. Also available are chess, dominos, checkers, backgammon, cards, baseballs and mitts, and boxing gloves. The hobby craft area permits you to order supplies from catalogues relating to the hobby, but the money to pay for them comes from your commissary fund.

Rehab/Counseling

There are programs for every type of addiction that can be claimed by an inmate. Campers, if in prison because of alcohol or drug involvement, must take a Drug Awareness Program, popularly known as DAP. It is mandatory throughout the system. Taking it can help eliminate going to such classes after you are released, when you go for driver's license renewal or for the reinstatement of your professional license.

The higher security FCIs and Penitentiaries also offer courses for sex offenders, a class of prisoners who are never sent directly to Camps.

All institutions also host programs for Gamblers (GA) and Alcoholics (AA), usually sponsored by inmates under the supervision of counselors or re-education personnel. If your PSI reports a substance abuse problem, you may qualify for an intensive rehab program which can reduce your sentence.

Religion

Nearly all prisons have chaplains available to serve the religious needs of the inmate population in general ways. Most prisons provide a Protestant and a Catholic chaplain on a full time basis, usually as a member of the staff, and contract out for the services of a rabbi or an imam when the number of Jewish and Moslem inmates makes that need appropriate. Wardens and administrators regard chaplains as a safety valve, able to relieve the pressure of confrontations between inmates or between inmates and the institution.

Chaplains usually are called upon to bring you the bad news from home, telling you that a family member is dangerously ill or has died. They also provide regular religious services and are available for one-on-one consultations.

Sanitation

This is an important matter in all prisons. There are usually a dozen or more rules to be adhered to. Some of them are not enforced, like card playing in the cube which never seems to be a problem, even though your cube or cell gets a bit messy. But if it causes a lot of disturbance, and other inmates complain, then the rule is there to be enforced.

Sex

Straight sex is nearly non-existent in prison. What is available is homosexual activity, but you should know that, if you get yourself involved in a relationship, you are treading on very thin ice. If you are caught, or "ratted out," you will be sent to a segregation cell and eventually transferred, either to an institution with a higher security level, or to another same-level institution with loss of your good time. Trying to make it with a guard is the quickest way to get into very serious trouble. The best advice is to use the celibate life to develop your long-neglected spiritual side from which you may have been distracted till now.

If abstinence is not what's on your mind, you can safely gratify your urges with self indulgence...either under the blanket or in the shower (unless you are in a group shower). It's suggested you be reticent here as well since other inmates enjoy poking fun at those they catch in the act.

If you worry about bending over to pick up a bar of soap in a group shower, squat. Unless you've sent out a signal you want to party, or an inmate gang wants to teach you a lesson for some infraction of inmate mores, you can bend safely. More women in prison means an escalation in the number of charges of sexual abuse. Like it or not, many U.S. women's prisons have male guards despite international rules discouraging the practice. Women can complain about sexual abuse in the army and leave. In prison, they can't leave and often see a worsening change in their conditions when they do complain. Pity the woman who thinks she can use seduction to win an "easier time" for long.

Smoking

Smokers in camps must learn to like the outdoors because that is where they can smoke. No smoking is permitted inside the buildings. Smokers violating this regulation can get a shot or be punished with "extra duty." In-Custody inmates can smoke in their cells.

Telephone calls

Telephones are in the housing units and outside of recreation or food service areas in the main buildings. Calls from all prisons are usually limited to 15 minutes and are monitored and recorded. Conducting business on the phone is a prohibited act. With the permission of your unit counselor, who allows you to use his phone, you may make unrecorded legal calls to your attorney.

Inmates can make phone calls by using coins, calling collect, or by pre-paying from money set aside in a special telephone fund. Coins and collect are becoming less optional as more of the institutions are requiring the pre-pay method. This method limits the inmate to a maximum of 20 telephone numbers, all of which must be identified as to name, city, state, and relationship to the inmate. The inmate receives a special billing number of his own which he punches into the phone at the sound of a special signal, after dialing the number of the party he wishes to reach. Money for these calls comes out of the money you bring with you to prison, the money you earn as a working inmate, and the money sent to you by friends or relatives. The commissary does this processing.

A benefit of the pre-pay method is that it costs less than the collect-call system. It also cuts off at 15 minutes, limiting the hogging of phones by some of the more burly and intimidating inmates, and greatly reducing the possibilities of argumentative confrontation between inmates over phone time abuse.

Television

Rumors always abound about removing outside television reception from various prisons. Cages do rattle, but both ways. Odds are in your favor, it's yours to view.

With few exceptions in all prison levels, everyone gets a chance to watch television. In some places, inmates control what is viewed in the television recreation rooms. In others, the administrators of the shift determine what is shown, at what volume, and at what hours. The lower the security level, the more inmate control. Some of the newer institutions, especially on the state level, permit television viewing in each cell where inmates are locked down for the night. These inmates pay cable fees from their commissary account.

There are usually at least two television rooms to a housing unit, with one designated as the sports TV room. All receivers are cable-connected and usually carry HBO programming.

State prisons are more apt to permit individual TV monitors. You buy them from the canteen or commissary. All institutions provide cable connections when available. Some charge you. Keep your set locked away when you are out of your cell. Guards will not rush to conduct "shake downs" because you're out a television set. Your set will turn up eventually since it carries your engraved registration number. If you are lucky, it will still be working.

Some camps limit the hours of television viewing; others do not. The only times you may not watch TV is when you have to be in your cube or cell at count times.

Unit Management System

This means "the team" — the camp administrator or the warden, the manager of your housing unit, the institutional case manager, a correctional counselor, a correctional officer, a camp secretary, an education representative and the psychologist.

The team interviews and classifies every new prisoner, usually within four weeks. The team sometimes sit together as a group or they do it separately. Inmates transferred from other institutions are teamed within 14 days of their arrival. Thereafter you will see team members at intervals of 90 days or 180 days, depending upon how much time you have to serve. The specific responsibilities of each of your team members doesn't affect you at this time, but you should be aware that they have a pecking order with the camp administrator or warden at the top.

Visiting

In most camps (the more crowded the camp or facility, the fewer the visiting hours), visits are permitted on weekends and on national holidays from 8:30 a.m. to 3:30 p.m. In all higher level institutions, visitors are permitted daily. Each prisoner is permitted a prescribed number of visits each month.

During your initial interview with your Counselor, you can participate in the preparation of a visiting list that includes immediate family members plus ten friends. Unapproved visitors are denied access to you. Visitors and you are expected to comply with a code of behavior. One camp manual gives the general idea: "Kissing and embracing upon arrival and departure is permitted within the bounds of good taste. Hand holding is permitted."

In some higher security facilities, visitors and inmates cannot touch, speaking into phones on opposite sides of a glass partition. Other facilities and camps have visiting rooms with guards present. Visiting rooms are usually crowded, and privacy does not exist. So, if you want to keep your business relatively private, you have to lower your voice a good bit. Many institutions have small areas within the visiting rooms set aside for the exclusive use of children, with television, toys, and child-size tables and chairs provided from the Inmate Benefit Fund (see Glossary).

Before and after each visit, inmates are subject to pat searches and random strip searches. In penitentiaries, visitors are also searched.

"Special" visits (such as visits from employers, investigators, and parole representatives) and "legal" visits (from an attorney) must be approved in advance by the Unit Team and authorized by the Camp or Prison Administrator.

First visits are usually traumatic. Tears flow. Let them. Families find you are well, look to be in one piece, and a lot of what they feared about prison life and its effect on you physically will be instantly dispelled. So don't postpone it. It's a healer for both prisoner and family.

33

Work

Without exception, all federal prisoners must work unless specifically excused by the institution's medical staff. Although the pay levels are low by any scale, you do get paid. This is the norm at all prisons.

There are two levels of pay in the institutions, each marked by different grades. The prison complex itself has four grades, starting at 12 cents an hour, moving up to 17 cents, 29 cents and finally to 40 cents an hour. UNICOR, the nickname for Prison Industries, is a big business within the prison system. It manufactures everything from coaxial cable to metal beds, furniture, clothing and room dividers, while also operating a complex warehouse distribution system. Workers in UNICOR start at 23 cents an hour and move up to $1.15 which is the fifth grade. UNICOR pays double for overtime.

Most inmates with committed fines are directed toward UNICOR employment, since the institution strives to have you work the fine off as much as you can by drawing a goodly amount of your monthly pay for that purpose. Other inmates seek UNICOR employment because it enables them to send money home where it may be sorely needed.

Jobs run from Monday through Friday, with weekends and holidays off. Days off may vary depending on the job. Food Services, for example, is a seven-day operation, and workers may get off only one day a week or two days that are not consecutive. Whatever the job, prisoners are required to put in a seven-and-a-half-hour shift each working day.

The higher security level institutions do more in-house construction work and have fully equipped carpentry and metal shops. The camps, especially those designated as satellites, seldom have need for such facilities.

But in all levels prisoners usually are assigned to landscaping, policing, pruning, weeding, grass cutting, tree cutting, shrub cleaning, road digging, sign posting, and ditch digging; or to work as an orderly, inside the administration building or in the laundry, rec, or education departments, or in the housing units and within the dormitories or ranges where you sleep; or to facilities, which includes the garage, power house, welding shops, and warehouses where you find work as a mechanic, gauge reader, welder, or warehouseman. Some inmates are given a test to earn a "government license" and are designated to drive vans, trucks, earth-moving, and grounds equipment around the compound or around the camp.

If they peg you round and put you in a round hole, so much the better. If they fit you into a square hole, in about sixty days you can write a "cop out" to your counselor, requesting a transfer to a job you would prefer, and odds are you will get it.

Playing It Safe

In prison, you can't choose the company you keep. Although the Prison Bureau tries to avoid putting the more violence-prone inmates in with the more genteel, there does occur some slippage as inmates work their way down from prisons of high-security to low-security FCI's and eventually to the camps.

Wherever you find yourself, the following rules will help you to stay out of trouble with both inmates and prison staff.

1. If a crowd is gathering, even on the recreation field, stay out of it.

2. Don't talk about your personal life or your case freely. You might give away information that could later be used as leverage against you.

3. Be courteous to guards, administration people, and anyone else employed by the BOP, but avoid becoming overly familiar with them. Some inmates may interpret anything more than a cordial relationship as a sign that you are an informer.

4. The commissary sells locks. If your cabinet can be locked up, do so, and leave it locked. Otherwise you may find yourself making repeated trips to the commissary to purchase the same items.

5. What you see, you don't see. Mind your own business. Walk away from fights. Don't carry tales, a sure way to earn an unsavory reputation.

6. Some institutions require you to reserve your phone time a day in advance. Despite this seemingly orderly process, many fights occur as some try to take advantage of phone time to cut into your 15 minutes. Just remember, it takes two to tango. Don't get into a quarrel. Walk away. The other guy will get his due sooner than you think.

7. TV tastes are as varied as the population. The majority rules, and sometimes the noise level overrides your ability to hear the show. It's better to leave than to fuss. You'll soon discover which viewing group to join in order to increase your enjoyment of TV time. Many fights occur between inmates over who decides what to watch.

8. After a while, you will find people you like to spend time with— birds of a feather. You might be able to maneuver eventually to sharing the same home range or be a bunk buddy.

9. Never complain about the behavior of another inmate or a hack. Either handle the problem yourself, or suffer it out. If the inmate is generally troublesome, he will eventually do himself in by challenging the system once too often.

10. Always be where you are supposed to be. If you are not, it must be because you have a hack's permission to be elsewhere.

11. You must always be at the proper place at count time. No excuses are acceptable for missing a count, unless you are lying on the sidewalk with a heart attack.

12. A worthwhile commissary purchase is a decent watch. Most of them are of good quality and are battery operated. Some even have alarms to remind you where you need to be at certain times of day.

13. There are times you will feel your case worker or your counselor isn't moving fast enough to help you with a personal problem or request. Be patient. Don't jump the command line. If they don't respond, send them a "cop out." If the cop out produces no satisfaction, submit a BP $8^1/_2$ for an administrative review . Only then, if necessary, submit a BP 9 to the warden or to the camp administrator. Going to the top directly is considered an affront to your case worker or counselor, an impression that can come back to you in frustrating ways.

Staying Sane

Make use of time. Take advantage of whatever programs are offered — take GED or college courses or vocational classes, participate in recovery groups or counselling if you have an addiction problem (alcohol, drug abuse, gambling), work for the Inmate Benefit Fund, join in the recreational offerings, etc. You'll feel better and time will pass more quickly if you stay as active as possible.

You'll be surprised at the initiative shown by some of your fellow inmates. You might do the same, if you are of the same mind. You will find they have gotten the education or recreation departments to approve them teaching a non-accredited course. Imagine taking a boating captain's navigation course from a licensed master skipper, or courses in how to set up your own business from proven entrepreneurs.

If you don't have knowledge you feel is worth sharing, you might take in some of the courses yourself. The institution will give you a diploma at the end of the course, showing you have participated in extra curricular programs. Looks good on your record.

Try to develop a project or goal for yourself, physically and mentally — and stick to the schedule you have laid out to reach that goal. You'll know that, as the days go by, you are accomplishing something that's important to you. Every institution has a walking track. Make the most of it. It keeps you fit, clears your head, and the company you find on the track can at times be entertaining and informative. If you are jogging or running, odds are you'll be alone. But if you are just brisk walking, there will be others you will catch up to whose company will make the miles speed by.

You might try to keep a daily journal. You would be surprised at how interesting it can become, particularly if you send it back to the family. It provides another way of sharing. Just such a beginning resulted in this guide!

Keep your hygiene level high. A clean bunk area and clean clothes and a neat appearance help to keep you sparkling mentally as well as physically.

Bait and Switch
and the Rumor Mill

Your time in prison will be better spent if you don't set yourself up for disappointments.

When you ask your case worker or counselor for furlough consideration as you've served the required amount of time in your sentence to make you eligible, be prepared for their ready response, "Of course, it's available to you!"

But know, as the time nears and your expectations grow, odds are you will instead be told a half dozen reasons why you have become ineligible at "this particular time."

Your first conversations with fellow inmates will be full of their assurances to you that Congress or your state legislature has under serious consideration legislation guaranteed to reduce the time you have to serve. They have folders full of letters to the editor, columnists' opinions or news stories related to such reductions.

Your last conversations with fellow inmates as you tick off the final days of your full sentence will be to assure them you fully share their optimism that such legislation is imminent and overdue. Weren't you told back then the tax paying public would no longer tolerate the continued expansion of wasteful prison facilities to relieve overcrowding?

For Your Family and Friends....

Tell them not to worry. You won't be lost in the federal system for any length of time. They can always find out where you are or to where you've been transferred by dialing the Federal Inmate Locator Service at 202-307-3126. Fifty states mean 50 different telephone numbers, but this same service is available from each.

Epilogue: "And this too shall pass..."

The best of luck to you. Do each day as it comes. And don't look ahead and count the days that remain. They too will pass, and you will find your way, not soon enough, out of the new world order and back to the more pleasant and familiar old order you left behind.

Never forget you were a prisoner. Whether you are on probation or parole or have paid your debt in full, you don't fully enjoy the status of presumed innocence of the other citizenry. Be careful of any situations which may lead to an involvement with the law at any level.

And do remember it is "pay back" time...no, not to your enemies, but your family. You want to make up the time you've been taken from them. Do this well, and all your other plans will fall into place.

APPENDIX A
GLOSSARY

This is a list of frequently used terms in prison. You will learn others while you are inside — such as *snitch* — which have obvious meanings that needs no explanation here.

Boot Camp

An alternative form of imprisonment, much like an intensive basic training program with the Marine Corps at Paris Island, which cuts off a lot of your sentence time. To qualify, you must be under 35.

BP9

BP9 is the last of several steps afforded you as you try to fight a "shot" in your records, or demonstrate that you have been denied access to a program that would end in early release, or that you were refused a furlough. The BP9 is a written appeal on a special form to the Warden — your supreme court!

Call Out

One of two daily bulletins posted on your housing unit bulletin board. If your name is on the call out, you are required to report on the following day to the place and at the time indicated and not to your regular duty.

Census

A census can be taken any time of the day or evening. The prison is instantly shut down, and every inmate is told to remain where he is. He is then questioned as to why he is where he is at that given moment of time, and — if he is not where he should be and does not have any cadre's permission to be there — he can get a shot.

Change Orders

Change orders are posted beside the call-out sheets on your bulletin board. If your name is listed, you will also notice what your old assignment was, what your new one is, and where and when to report.

Sometimes seeing your name on that sheet is good news, particularly when it is the job change you had requested. Other times, not so, since your job may be changed to a less pleasant one in order to punish you.

Commissary

Your prison supermarket and clothing store.

Contraband

Anything found on your person or your locker that was not approved by R & D, nor available in the Commissary. It will be confiscated. If the offense is considered serious, it could mean your removal to a higher security prison.

Cop Out

A cop out is the first step in the administrative remedy process. It is a request form used for various purposes — to see the doctor or the dentist or one of the department heads. It is easily used and is the main means of written requests from inmates to the cadre.

Count Time or Count Down

When you hear one of those terms, you know it is time to be in your cubicle or cell. If you are not, the authorities will assume you are trying to escape. The consequences are not good.

Diesel Tour

When you choose to let the marshals take you from court to the prison to which you are designated, or when you are being transferred from one institution to another because of misbehavior or at your request, you are transported by buses that are in no particular hurry. You may be left at one institution or another for any number of days until you are picked up to be taken to another temporary stop, etc., until you get to your final destination. It is not a pleasant trip.

Furlough

A furlough permits you to leave the prison facility for a day or two without an escort for family emergencies. On some occasions, you may actually be allowed to go into the nearest town on errands for the prison. When inmates are within 60 days of being released, they are sometimes given a furlough to become reacquainted with their families.

Hack

Hacks are custodial officers, the people in charge of making sure you stay in prison and abide by the rules. They enforce all rules and regulations. What a hack says receives first preference in what happens to you, no matter how valuable a worker you might be in the department to which you have been assigned. If a hack says you have broken a rule that they consider serious and hits you with a high-degree shot, you can be whisked to a segregation cell and eventually diesel toured to a higher security facility.

Halfway House

A stay at a halfway house is one of the programs offered to inmates to shorten their stay at prison facilities. It is really a prison of sorts, but you are allowed to work at a job and visit your family, as long as you are back at the house by 9:00 p.m. free of alcohol and drugs. The halfway-house privilege is granted to inmates near the end of their sentence if their behavior has been good. The maximum stay is six months.

House Arrest

This is the most lenient of all early-release programs. You remain at home under electronic surveillance.

Inmate Benefit Fund. (IBF)

Most older institutions have in place an Inmate Benefit Fund, an umbrella non-profit group designed to raise money from various projects approved by the Administration. The children's section in the visiting rooms are often furnished from funds provided by their efforts. The IBF also act as the starter-up of other organizations such as the inmate Jay-Cees. If you want to get involved in these organizations, speak to your counselor.

Main Line

That is the line in chow hall that is open to the general inmate population. The food is always better in the short line.

PSI

Your Pre-Sentence Investigation report is prepared by your Probation Officer. It de-scribes how you are viewed by your prison administration team.

R & D

Receiving and Dismissal is the first place you visit when you arrive at prison and are strip-searched for the first time, fingerprinted and have your picture taken. It is also the final place you will be before going home after your final strip-search. Your re-cords are kept here.

Shank

This is any object that can be construed as a weapon by custodial officers. Inmates in higher security facilities love to make shanks and are totally ingenious in fabricating weapons out of apparently harmless items.

Short Line

This refers to the early mess hour reserved for kitchen staff and those kitchen workers who have finished their work or have the day off. Food here is superior to what is served on the main line, and the quantity offered is not limited.

Shot

A shot is a disciplinary report which finds its way into your record. If appeals fail, a shot can affect how much of your prison sentence you will have to serve, and whether or not you will lose your right to a furlough for which you will have otherwise qualified.

Team

Administration personnel who process you through the system and are your team. They are your judge and jury when it comes to determining whether you will be given an opportunity to take part in one of the alternative prison programs such as half-way houses, furloughs, etc.

APPENDIX B
FEDERAL CORRECTIONAL
INSTITUTIONS AND CAMPS

Here they are, those federal prisons that are currently open and those planned. Study the descriptions on the following pages, compare, and try to get your judge to send you to your choice. The source of the information is the Federal Bureau of Prisons, U.S. Department of Justice, 320 First Street, Washington, D.C. 20534.

Federal Bureau of Prisons Regional Offices:

Central Office: 320 First Street, N.W., Washington, D.C. 20534. 202-307-3198

Mid-Atlantic Regional Office: Junction Business Park, 10010 Junction Dr., Suite 100-N, Annapolis Junction, MD 20701. 301/317-3100

North Central Regional Office: Gateway Complex Tower II, 8th Floor, 4th and State Ave., Kansas City, KS 66101.-2492. 913/621-3939

Northeast Regional Office: U.S. Customs House, 7th Floor, 2nd and Chestnut Sts., Philadelphia, PA 19106. 215/597-6317

South Central Regional Office: 4211 Cedar Springs Rd., Suite 300, Dallas, TX 75219. 214/767-9700

Southeast Regional Office: 523 McDonough Blvd., S.E., Atlanta, GA 30315. 404/624-5202

Western Regional Office: 7950 Dublin Blvd., 3rd Floor, Dublin, CA 94568. 510/803-4700

Abbreviations:

ADMAX	Administrative Maximum	FCC	Federal Correctional Complex
FCI	Federal Correctional Institution	FDC	Federal Detention Center
FMC	Federal Medical Center	FPC	Federal Prison Camp
FTC	Federal Transfer Center	LSCI	Low Security Correctional Institution
MCC	Metropolitan Correctional Center	MCFP	Medical Center for Federal Prisoners
MDC	Metropolitan Detention Center	USP	United States Penitentiary

FPC Alderson
Box B, Alderson, West Virginia 24910
304-445-2901, Fax: 304-445-2675
Federal Prison Camp, Mid-Atlantic Region
    Accredited
    Security Level: Minimum/Female
    Judicial District: Southern District of West Virginia.
    Capacity: Rated-688

Accreditation Status indicates whether an institution is accredited by the Commission on Accreditation for Corrections. The process of accreditation provides an additional level of assurance that Federal prisons offer decent living conditions, provide adequate programs and services, and safeguard inmate rights by ensuring compliance with the more than 400 standards developed by the Commission. Additionally, the U.S. Medical Center for Federal Prisoners in Springfield, Missouri, the Federal Medical Center in Rochester, Minnesota, and the Coswell Medical Centers in Fort Worth, Texas, are accredited by the Joint Commission on Accreditation of Hospitals.

Overview: Opened in 1927 as the Federal Reformatory for Women, FPC Alderson was the first institution for female Federal offenders. The inmate population represents all States and several foreign countries, with an age range from 19 to 71.

Location: In the foothills of the Allegheny Mountains, 270 miles southwest of Washington, D.C., 12 miles south of Interstate 64, off State Highway 3. The area is served by the Greenbrier Valley Airport in Lewisburg (17 miles from the facility), airports in Beckley (50 miles away) and Roanoke, Virginia (113 miles away), Amtrak, and Greyhound.

FPC Allenwood
PO Box 1000, Montgomery, Pennsylvania 17752
717-547-1641, Fax 717-547-1504
Northeast Region

Security Level: Minimum/Male

Judicial District: Middle District of Pennsylvania

Capacity, December 1993: 567

Location: 200 miles north of Washington, D.C. and 7 miles south of Williamsport, Pennsylvania. 8 miles north of Interstate 80, off State Highway 15. The area is served by the Williamsport-Lycoming County Airport and bus lines.

FCI Allenwood Low
PO Box 1500, White Deer, Pennsylvania 17887
717-547-1990, Fax: 717-547-1740
Northeast Region

Security Level: Low/Male

Judicial District: Middle District of Pennsylvania

Capacity, December 1993: 992

FCI Allenwood Medium
PO. Box 2500, White Deer, Pennsylvania 17887
717-547-7950, Fax 717-547-7035
Northeast Region

Security Level: Medium/Male

Judicial District: Middle District of Pennsylvania

Capacity, December 1993: 839

USP Allenwood
PO Box 3500, White Deer, Pennsylvania 17887
717-547-0963, Fax 717-547-0983

Security Level: High/Male

Judicial District: Middle District of Pennsylvania

Capacity, December 1993: 640

FCI Ashland
Ashland, Kentucky 41101
606-928-6414, Fax: 606-358-8552
Federal Correctional Institution, Mid-Atlantic Region

Accredited

Security Level: Medium/Male (adjacent Minimum/Male camp)

Judicial District: Eastern District of Kentucky

Capacity: Rated-662. Adjacent camp: Rated-296

Overview: Opened in 1940, FCI Ashland houses male offenders with sentences ranging from 6 months to life. The average inmate is 35 years old serving a 12 year sentence. Satellite Camp: Opened in 1990, FPC Ashland houses minimum security inmates, who are employed in maintenance positions in support of the main institution.

Location: In the highlands of northeastern Kentucky, 125 miles east of Lexington and 5 miles southwest of Ashland. On State Route 716,1 mile west of U.S. 60.

USP Atlanta
601 McDonough Blvd., S.E. Atlanta, Georgia 30315
404-635-5100, Fax: 404-331-2137
U.S. Penitentiary, Southeast Region

Security Level: Administrative/Male (Adjacent Minimum/Male camp)

Judicial District: Northern District of Georgia

Capacity: Rated-1,429. Adjacent camp: Rated-488

Overview: Opened in 1902, USP Atlanta primarily held Cuban detainees from 1980-1987; it was reconstructed following the 1987 disturbance and currently houses male inmates of all security levels, holdovers, and pretrial inmates. New building added 199S. Houses detention pre-trial inmates. Capacity 370. Satellite Camp: Opened in 1984, FPC Atlanta serves as a satellite facility to the main institution and houses primarily minimum-custody, nonviolent offenders.

Location: In the southeast corner of Atlanta, at the junction of Boulevard and McDonough Streets. Off Interstate 7 (Exit 88), Interstate 20 (Exit 26), or Interstate 285 (Exit 39). Atlanta is served by Hartsfield International Airport and Greyhound.

FCI Bastrop
Box 730 Bastrop, Texas 78602
512-304-0117; Fax. 512-304-0117
Federal Correctional Institution, South Central Region

Accredited

Security level: Low/Male (adjacent Minimum/Male camp)

Judicial District: Western District of Texas

Capacity: Rated: 793, Camp: 122

Overview: Opened in 1979, FCI Bastrop houses male offenders of all ages primarily from the south central United States.

Location: 30 miles southeast of Austin, 8 miles south of Elgin, and 8 miles north of Bastrop. Off Highway 9S. The area is served by Austin Municipal Airport (27 miles from the facility).

FCC Beaumont
PO Box 26015, Beaumont, TX 77726-6015
409-840-2002; FCI Low-409-727-8172; Fax 409-626-3401
South Central Region

Opened in 1996, this Federal Correctional Complex consists of four institutions (minimum, low, medium, and high security). It includes a shared services administration building to include areas such as employee development, facility maintenance, financial management, powerhouse, safety services and warehouse facilities. Approx. staffing 1,000, 60% from local region.

Rated inmate capacity: Low security, 1,536; high security, 960; medium, 1,152; and minimum (camp), 512. Spread over 900 acres within Beaumont City limits, complex construction cost $250 million. Annual operating budget estimated at $100 million.

FCI Beckley
PO Box 1280 Beaver, WV 25813
304-255-7189, Fax:304-256-4955
Mid-Atlantic Region

Judicial District: Southern District of West Virginia
Security Level: Medium/male (adjacent minimum/male camp)
Rated capacity: 1,152; Camp, 390.
Opened 1995.

FCI Big Spring
Big Spring, Texas 79720
915-263-6699, Fax 915-268-6860
Federal Correctional Institution, South Central Region

Accredited
Security Level: Low/Male (adjacent Minimum/Male camp)
Judicial District: Northern District of Texas
Capacity: Rated 655. Satellite camp: Rated 144
Overview: Opened in 1979 as a prison camp, FCI Big Spring is part of the former Webb Air Force Base. It was converted to a low security facility in September 1990. It houses male offenders of all ages, primarily from Texas, the most common offenses being drug offenses. Satellite Camp Opened in spring 1992, FPC Big Spring houses minimum-security male offenders. The camp provides a labor force in support of the main institution as well as to local Federal agencies.
Location: Midway between Dallas and El Paso on the southwest edge of Big Spring. At the intersection of Interstate 20 and U.S. Highway 80. The area is served by Midland/Odessa Airport (50 miles from Big Spring), a small municipal airport within the Big Spring Industrial Park, and Greyhound.

FPC Boron
P.O. Box 500 Boron, California 93596
619-762-6230, Fax: 619-762-5719
Federal Prison Camp, Western Region

Accredited
Security Level: Minimum/Male
Judicial District: Central District of California
Capacity: Rated-439

Overview: Opened in 1979, FPC Boron is a former Air Force radar station. It serves as a buffer between larger institutions and the community, housing primarily first-time and short-term offenders from California and Nevada. A community involvement program is available to the inmates.

Location: In the Mojave Desert of Southern California, 37 miles west of Barstow and 75 miles north of San Bernardino. Off State Highway 395, 6 miles north of the junction with Highway 58. The area is served by Ontario International Airport (90 miles from the facility), Los Angeles International Airport (110 miles away), Amtrak (service to Barstow), and Greyhound.

MDC Brooklyn
100 29th Street, Brooklyn, NY 11232
718-832-1039; Fax 718-832-4225
Metropolitan Detention Center, Northeast Region

Security Level: Administrative/Male/Female

Rated capacity: 578

Judicial District: Eastern District of New York

Overview: MDC Brooklyn is designed to house pretrial and unsentenced detainees (both male and female) appearing in Federal courts in the Eastern District of New York.

Location: At Bush Terminal in Brooklyn, bounded by 29th and 30th Streets to the north and south and by 2nd and 3rd Avenues to the west and east. New York City is served by LaGuardia, Kennedy, and Newark international airports.

FPC Bryan
P.O. Box 2197 Bryan, Texas 77805-4951
409-823-1879, Fax: 409-775-5681
Federal Prison Camp, South Central Region

Security Level: Minimum/Female (adjacent Minimum/Female ICC)

Judicial District: Southern District of Texas

Capacity: Rated-720. ICC: Rated-82.

Overview Opened in 1988, FPC Bryan houses female offenders primarily from Texas and the surrounding States. Intensive Confinement Center: The ICC, which opened in July 1992, will house 100 minimum-security inmates in 2 open-bay areas in a highly structured program of work education, physical training, and life skills development

Location: 9S miles north of Houston and 165 miles south of Dallas. In the town of Bryan at the intersection of Ursuline Avenue and 23rd Street. The area is served by Easterwood Airport in College Station, connecting through Houston Intercontinental and Dallas-Fort Worth Airports.

FCI Butner
P.O. Box 1000 Butner, North Carolina 27509
919-575-4541, Fax: 919-575-6341
Federal Correctional Institution, Mid Atlantic Region

Accredited

Security Level: Low & Medium/Administrative/Male (adjacent Minimum/Male camp). Low Security on line 1995. Rated capacity 992. Old N.C. Highway 75; 919-575-4999. Medium capacity rated 513

Judicial District: Eastern District of North Carolina.

FCIC (Low): Mission Mental health. Rated capacity 800.

Capacity: Rated 513. Adjacent camp: Rated 100.

Overview: Opened in 1976, FCI Butner functions as an inpatient psychiatric hospital and as a medium-security facility for inmates serving varied and complex sentences. Inmates are primarily from the southeast with ages ranging from 18 to 71 . Satellite Camp: Activated in 1991, FPC Butner houses minimum-secunty male offenders, most of whom provide services to the main institution.   Location: Located near the Research Triangle area of Durham, Raleigh, and Chapel Hill. 5 miles off Interstate 8 on Old Highway 75. The area is served by the Raleigh-Durham Airport.

Federal Medical Center Carswell (East)
I Street, Building 3000
Fort Worth, TX 76127-7066
817-782-4000, Fax. 817-782-4875
>   Female Population

Federal Medical Center Carswell (West)
(Former FCI)
3150 Horton Rd., Fort Worth, TX
817-535-1211
>   Male population

MCC Chicago
71 West Van Buren
Chicago, Illinois 60667
312-322-0567, Fax: 312-322-0565
Metropolitan Correctional Center, North Central Region
>   Accredited
>   Security Level: Administrative/Male/Female
>   Judicial District: Northern District of Illinois
>   Capacity: Rated-411
>   Overview: Opened in 1975, MCC Chicago is a 26-story triangular structure housing pretrial detainees, inmates awaiting sentencing and designation, sentenced holdovers on writ, convicted inmates who comprise a work cadre, and INS detainees.
>   Location: Located near the U.S. District Court in downtown Chicago, at the intersection of Clark and Van Buren Streets. Chicago is served by Midway and O'Hare Airports (Midway is closest to MCC Chicago), Amtrak, and Greyhound.

FCI Coleman (medium)
811 N.E. 54th Terrace, Coleman, FL 33521-8999
352-330-3200
>   Medium security, male
>   Rated capacity: 1,152.

FCI Coleman (low)
868 N.E. 54th Terrace, Coleman, FL 33521-8999
352-330-3100
> Low security, male
> Rated capacity: 1,536.

FCI Coleman Administration
846 N.E. 54th Terrace, Coleman, FL 33521-8999
352-330-3000
> FPC Coleman (352-330-3200) opened late 1997. Central administration building responsible for all shared supervision prison complexes.
> Female only
> Capacity 512
> Located south of Ocala, FL, 70 miles from Orlando.

FCI Cumberland
14601 Burbridge RD, SE Cumberland, Maryland 21502
301-784-1000; Fax 301-784-1008
> Security Level: Medium; Capacity: Rated 768. Adjacent camp: Security Level: Minimum; Rated: 256
> Male
> Location: Off Highway 68, Cumberland. Served by Cumberland Municipal Airport.

FCI Danbury
Danbury, Connecticut 06811-6471
203-746-6471; Fax. 203-312-3110
Federal Correctional Institution, Northeast Region
> Security Level: Low Female (adjacent Minimum/Female camp)
> Judicial District: District of Connecticut
> Capacity: Rated-508. Adjacent camp: Rated-178
> Overview: Opened in 1940. Offenders have been convicted of narcotics violations and property crimes. The institution uses a double fence and structural design as the primary physical security. Satellite Camp: Opened in 1982. FPC Danbury houses short-term low-security females primarily from the northeast U.S.
> Location: Southwestern Connecticut, 70 miles from NY City. 3 miles north of Danbury on State Rte 37. Served by Westchester County Airport (45 minutes away), New York City airports (90 minutes away, and Bonanza bus lines.

FCI Dublin (FCI Pleasanton)
8th Street, Camp Parks, Dublin, CA 94568
510-833-7500; Fax 510-833-7599
> Security Level: Low Female (adjacent Minimum Male camp)
> Judicial District: Northern District of California
> Capacity (December 1993): 810. Adjacent Camp: 299
> Overview: Opened in 1974, FCI Pleasanton houses female offenders primarily from the western U.S. An FDC opened in 1989 houses pretrial and pre-sentence offenders in custody of the U.S. Marshals Service. Satellite Camp: Opened in 1990, FPC Pleasanton houses minimum-security female offenders. The facility, located on Camp Parks military base, provides inmate labor to support the base, the FCI, and the FDC.

Location: 20 miles southeast of Oakland. Off Interstate 580 (Hopyard/Doughtery Road exit, proceed east to the Camp Parks Army Base). The area is served by San Francisco and Oakland airport.

FPC Duluth
P.O. Box 1400, Duluth, Minnesota 55814
218-722-8634, Fax: 218-733-4701
Federal Prison Camp, North Central Region

Accredited

Security Level: Minimum/Male

Judicial District: District of Minnesota

Capacity: Rated-885

Overview: Opened in 1983, FPC Duluth was formerly Duluth Air Force Base. Inmates are primarily from the north central states.

Location: On the southwestern tip of Lake Superior, halfway between Minneapolis-St. Paul and the U.S.-Canadian border. 7 miles north of Duluth, off Highway 53 at Stebner Road. Duluth is served by Duluth International Airport and Greyhound.

FPC Eglin
Eglin Air Force Base, Florida 32542
850-882-8522, Fax: 850-729-8261
Federal Prison Camp, Southeast Region

Accredited

Security Level: Minimum/Male

Judicial District: Northern District of Florida

Capacity: Rated-800

Overview: Opened in 1962, FPC Eglin houses male offenders primarily from the southeastern U.S. who do not have records of escape, violence, sexual offenses, or major medical/psychiatric problems. Inmates serve as an auxiliary work force for Eglin AFB.

Location: In northwest Florida's panhandle, 46 miles east of Pensacola on Eglin Air Force Base. The area is served by Pensacola Airport and Greyhound, and Eglin AFB has an on-site airstrip.

FPC El Paso
P.O. Box 16300 El Paso, Texas 79906-0300
915-566-1271, Fax: 915-540-6165
Federal Prison Camp, South Central Region

Security Level: Minimum/Male

Judicial District: Western District of Texas

Capacity: Rated-308

Overview: Opened in 1989, FPC El Paso is located on Biggs Army Air Field at the Fort Bliss Army Post. It houses offenders primarily from the southeastern/ southwestern U.S. who do not have records of escape, violence, sexual offenses, or major medical/psychiatric problems. Inmates serve as an auxiliary work force for Fort Bliss.

Location: The city of El Paso is located at the Texas border with Mexico and New Mexico, 30 miles east of Las Cruces, New Mexico, and 370 miles west of

Midland, Texas. The facility is located on Fort Bliss, about 5 miles northeast from the Biggs Field entrance on Sgt. Simms road. El Paso is served by El Paso International Airport, Amtrak, and Greyhound.

FCI El Reno
P.O. Box 1000 El Reno, Oklahoma 73036-1000
404-262-4875, Fax: 404-262-6266
Federal Correctional Institution, South Central Region

Accredited

Security Level: Medium/Male (adjacent Minimum/Male camp)

Judicial District: Western District of Oklahoma

Capacity: Rated-740. Adjacent camp: Rated-216.

Overview: Opened in 1933 on part of the former Fort Reno Military Reservation, FCI El Reno serves as a hub of inmate movement for the Federal Prison System. Inmates are male offenders from Texas and nearby states. Satellite Camp: Opened in 1980, FPC El Reno houses minimum-security inmates who are employed on its 3,000 acre farm providing beef and milk for El Reno and 8 other Federal institutions.

Location: 30 miles west of Oklahoma City. Off Interstate 40 (Country Club Exit, 2 miles north to Sunset Drive, then west for 2 miles) The area is served by Will Rogers World Airport in Oklahoma City.

FCI Elkton
PO Box 89, 8730 Scroggs Rd, Elkton, Ohio 44415
330-424-7448; Fax. 330-424-4539

Security Level: Low/Male (adjacent Minimum/Male Camp)

Judicial District: Northern Ohio

Capacity: FCI:500, Camp 256

Location: In Northeastern Ohio, less than an hour from Pittsburgh, Youngstown and Canton. The area is served by the international airport in Pittsburgh and regional airports in Youngstown and Canton, Amtrak, and commercial bus lines.

FCI Englewood
9595 W. Quincy Ave., Littleton, Colorado 80123
303-985-1566; Fax: 303 763-2553
Federal Correctional Institution, North Central Region

Accredited

Security Level: Medium/Administrative/Male (adjacent Administrative/Male and Minimum/Male camp).

Judicial District: District of Colorado

Capacity: Rated-475. Adjacent camp: Rated-87.

Overview: Opened in 1940, FCI Englewood houses both sentenced and unsentenced male inmates. A detention center, which is separate from the correctional institution, primarily houses Cuban detainees and unsentenced inmates. Satellite Camp: Opened in 1990, FPC Englewood serves as a satellite facility to the main institution. It houses minimum-security male offenders primarily from the western United States.

Location: 15 miles southwest of Denver. Off Interstate 285. The area is served by the Denver Airport.

FCI Estill
100 Prison Rd., Estill, SC 29918
803-625-4607; Fax 803-625-3139
Federal Correctional Institution, Mid-Atlantic Region

> Security Level: Medium/Male (adjacent Minimum/Male camp)
>
> Capacity: 768; Camp: 256
>
> Judicial District: District of South Carolina
>
> Overview: The institution was activated in the spring of 1993. Camp inmates provide services for the main institution.
>
> Location: In Hampton County, South Carolina, off State Road 531 about 3 miles south of the town of Estill. The area is served by the Savannah, Georgia, airport.

FCI Fairton
P.O. Box 280 Fairton, New Jersey 08320
609-453-1177, Fax: 609-453-4015
Federal Correctional Institution, Northeast Region

> Security Level: Medium/Male (adjacent Minimum/Male camp)
>
> Judicial District: District of New Jersey
>
> Capacity: Rated-765. Adjacent camp: Rated-65.
>
> Overview: Opened in 1990, FCI Fairton houses male offenders primarily from the northeastern U.S. A pretrial detention center is in operation, with bed space for 124 inmates. Satellite Camp: Opened in January 1992, FPC Fairton houses minimum-security inmates who will be employed on landscape and institution support details.
>
> Location: In south central New Jersey, 50 miles southeast of Philadelphia and 40 miles southwest of Atlantic City. Off Interstate 55. The area is served by Philadelphia International Airport, Atlantic City Airport, and Millville Municipal Airport.

ADX Florence
P.O. Box 7500, 5880 State Highway 67, South Florence, CO 81290
719-784-9454; Fax 719-784-5130

> Opened 1994. Administrative/Male.

USP Florence (Administrative maximum)
719-784-9464; Fax. 719-784-5157

> Rated capacity: 490.

FCI Florence
719-784-9100; Fax. 719-784-9504

> Security: Medium Male; Capacity: 744
>
> Camp Florence Security: Medium Male; Capacity: 512
>
> Location: 45 miles south of Colorado Springs, Colorado, and 30 miles west of Pueblo, Colorado. Take State Highway 115 from Colorado Springs or U.S. Highway 50 from Pueblo to State Highway 115. Turn south at the intersection of State Highway 115 and State Highway 67 in Florence. (Left at Hardee's.) Go about 2 miles south of Florence. The area is served by the Pueblo and Colorado Springs airports and by commercial buses.

FCI Forrest City
PO Box 7000 Forrest City Arkansas 72335
870-630-6000; Fax. 870-630-6250
  Security level: Low/Male
  Judicial District: Eastern Arkansas
  Capacity: 1536, Staff: 303
  Location: In eastern Arkansas, between Little Rock (85 miles west) and Memphis
  (45 miles east), and near Interstate 40. The region is served by air and rail in
  Memphis, and Forrest City is directly served by commercial bus lines.

FCI Fort Dix
PO Box 38, Fort Dix, NJ 08640
609-723-1000; Fax: 609-723-6847
  Security Level: Low/Male
  Judicial District: New Jersey
  Capacity: 3,683
  East and West Compounds Location: Approximately 45 miles northeast of
  Philadelphia, off exit 8 of the New Jersey Turnpike.

FMC Fort Worth
3150 Horton Road Fort Worth, Texas 76119-5996
817-534-8400, Fax: 817-413-3350
Federal Correctional Institution, South Central Region
  Accredited
  Security Level: Low/Administrative/Male
  Capacity: Rated-1,132
  Judicial District: Northern District of Texas
  Overview: Opened in 1971, FCI Fort Worth houses male inmates and provides
  specialized programs for inmates who have medical and drug/alcohol abuse
  treatment needs. The institution has 24-hour hospital coverage.
  Location: In North Central Texas, southeast of Fort Worth. North of Interstate 20
  and east of Interstate 35. Fort Worth is served by Dallas/Fort Worth International
  Airport, Amtrak, and Greyhound.

FCI Greenville
PO BOX 4000, Greenville, IL 62246
618-664-6200; Fax 618-664-6398
  Rated Capacity: 750
  Security Level: Medium/male
  Adjacent camp: Minimum/ male. Capacity: 256
  Location: By I-70, 50 miles east of St. Louis, MO. Served by St. Louis Airport.

MDC Guaynabo
P.O. Box 2146 San Juan, Puerto Rico 00922
809-749-4880, Fax: 809-749-4363
Metropolitan Detention Center, Southeast Region
  Security Level: Administrative/Male/Female
  Judicial District: District of Puerto Rico
  Capacity: 932

Overview: The institution, the first outside the continental U.S., was opened in November 1992.

Location: 1,250 miles southeast of Miami, Florida. 6 miles west of San Juan, Puerto Rico; off Highway 22 at the intersection of Road 165 and 128. The area is served by San Juan International Airport.

FCI Jesup
2600 Highway 301, South Jesup, Georgia 31545
912-427-0870, Fax: 912-427-1125
Federal Correctional Institution, Southeast Region

Security Level: Medium/Male (adjacent Minimum/Male camp). 45 Judicial District: Southern District of Georgia.

Capacity: Rated-744. Adjacent camp: Rated-508.

Overview: Houses male offenders primarily from southeastern U.S. Satellite Camp: Opened in 1989, FPC Jesup houses minimum-security male offenders, most of whom provide services to the main institution.

Location: Southeast Georgia on Rte 301, 65 mi. southwest of Savannah, 40 mi. northwest of Brunswick, 105 mi. northwest of Jacksonville. Served by Jacksonville and Savannah International Airports, Brunswick Airport.

FCI La Tuna
P.O. Box 1000, Highway 20, TX 88021
915-886-3422, Fax: 915-886-4977
Federal Correctional Institution, South Central Region

Accredited

Security Level: Low/male (adjacent Minimum/Male camp)

Judicial District: Western District of Texas

Capacity: Rated-556. Adjacent camp: Rated-246.

Overview: Opened in 1932, FCI La Tuna houses offenders from western Texas, New Mexico, Arizona, Colorado, Wyoming, and Southern Utah. 58.5 percent of the inmate population are Mexican and South and Central American nationals. Satellite Camp: Opened in 1978, FPC La Tuna serves as a satellite facility to the main institution. It houses minimum security male offenders.

Location: On the Texas/New Mexico border adjacent to Mexico, 20 miles north of El Paso. Off Interstate 10 on State Highway 20. The area is served by El Paso International Airport.

USP Leavenworth
1500 Metropolitan, Leavenworth, K5 66048
913-682-8700, Fax: 913-682-0041
U.S. Penitentiary, North Central Region

Security Level: High/Male (adjacent Minimum/Male camp)

Judicial District: District of Kansas

Capacity: Rated-1,201. Adjacent camp: Rated-398.

Overview: Opened in 1906, USP Leavenworth was the site of the first Federal prison. In 1895, Congress transferred the military prison at Fort Leavenworth to the Department of Justice. When the War Department objected, Congress authorized 1,000 acres adjacent to the prison for a new penitentiary to confine 1,200 inmates. USP Leavenworth houses adult male offenders, primarily from

Midwestern and western States, and Cuban detainees. Satellite Camp: Opened in 1960, FPC Leavenworth serves as a satellite facility to the main institution. It houses minimum-security male offenders.

Location: 25 miles north of Kansas City. On Highway 73. The area is served by Kansas City International Airport (15 miles from the facility).

USP Lewisburg
R.D. 5, Lewisburg, PA 17837
717-523-1251, Fax: 717-524-5805
U.S. Penitentiary, Northeast Region

Security Level: High/Male (adjacent Minimum/Male camp and Minimum/Male Interstate Confinement Center)

Judicial District: Middle District of Pennsylvania.

Capacity: Rated-809. ICC: Rated-240.

Overview: Opened in 1932, USP Lewisburg is the only high security Federal penitentiary on the East Coast. Inmates are primarily from the New England and Mid-Atlantic States. Satellite Camp: A new 352-bed minimum-security camp opened in 1992. Intensive Confinement Center: This 180-bed facility opened in 1991. It houses minimum-security male offenders in a no-frills, highly structured program of work, education, physical training, and life skills development.

Location: In rural central Pennsylvania outside the town of Lewisburg, 200 miles from Washington, D.C., and 170 miles from Philadelphia. 6 miles south of Interstate 80, 2 miles off U.S. Route 15. The area is served by Williamsport Airport.

FMC Lexington
3301 Leestown Road
Lexington, Kentucky 40511
606-255-6812, Fax: 606-253-8821
Federal Medical Center, Mid-Atlantic Region

Lexington FPC

Accredited

Security Level: Administrative/Female

Judicial District: Eastern District of Kentucky

Capacity: Rated-1,106

Overview: Opened in 1974, FMC Lexington formerly was a U.S. Public Health Service facility. It houses female offenders whose average length of stay is 2.5 years. A 100-bed hospital accepts inmate referrals from throughout the U.S.

Location: 7 miles north of Lexington on U.S. Highway 421. Lexington is served by Blue Grass Field Airport and Greyhound.

USP Lompoc
3901 Klein Boulevard, Lompoc, California 93436
805-735-2771, Fax: 805-737-0295
U.S. Penitentiary, Western Region

Accredited

Security Level: High/Male (adjacent Minimum/Male camp)

Judicial District: Central District of California

Capacity: Rated-980. ICC capacity 80.

Overview: Opened in 1959, USP Lompoc houses inmates serving long sentences for sophisticated offenses. Satellite Camp: Provides services to USP and FCI Lompoc, Vandenberg AFB, and farm and community service projects. Rated: 276. Location: 175 miles northwest of Los Angeles, adjacent to Vandenberg Air Force Base off Route 1. The area is served by Santa Barbara Airport (25 miles south), Santa Maria Airport (25 miles north), and Greyhound.

FCI Lompoc
3600 Guard Road Lompoc, California 93436
805-736-4154, Fax: 805-736-7163
Federal Correctional Institution, Western Region
   Security Level: Low/Male.
   3436 Judicial District: Central District of California
   Capacity: Rated-472
   Overview: Opened in 1970 as a Federal Prison Camp, FCI Lompoc was converted to a low-security facility in 1990. It houses male offenders, primarily from California, Arizona, and Nevada, many of whom are serving their first period of confinement.
   Location: 175 miles northwest of Los Angeles, adjacent to Vandenberg Air Force Base. The area is served by Santa Barbara Airport (60 miles south), Santa Maria Airport (25 miles north), and Greyhound.

FCI Loretto
P.O. Box 1000
Loretto, Pennsylvania 15940
814-472-4140, Fax: 814-472-6046
Federal Correctional Institution, Northeast Region
   Security Level: Low/Male
   Judicial District: Western District of Pennsylvania
   Capacity: Rated-477; FPC Loretto: 106
   Overview: Opened in 1984, FCI Loretto is a former Catholic seminary built in 1960. It houses inmates primarily from the northeast, most of whom are first offenders serving between 5 and 14 years, in the 33-39 age group. The majority of offenders are serving sentences for violating drug laws. A perimeter fence was constructed in 1990 that increased the security level.
   Location: In southwest Pennsylvania between Altoona and Johnstown, 90 miles east of Pittsburgh. Off Route 22, midway between Interstate 80 and the Pennsylvania Turnpike via Route 220. The area is served by Pittsburgh International Airport, Amtrak, and Greyhound. Altoona and Johnstown are served by commuter airlines.

MDC Los Angeles
535 N. Alameda Street Los Angeles, California 90012
213-485-0439, Fax: 213-626-5801
Metropolitan Detention Center, Western Region
   Security Level: Administrative/Male/Female
   Judicial District: Central District of California
   Capacity: Rated-728
   Overview: Opened in 1988, MDC Los Angeles houses a small work cadre, pretrial and pre-sentence inmates from California, and holdovers from other parts of the country.

Location: In downtown Los Angeles, off the Hollywood Freeway (Highway 101) on the comer of Alameda and Aliso Streets. The area is served by Los Angeles International Airport and Amtrak.

FCI Manchester
P.O. Box 3000, Manchester, KY 40962
606-598-1900, Fax: 606-599-4115
Federal Correctional Institution, Mid-Atlantic Region

Security Level: Medium/Male (adjacent Minimum/Male camp)

Judicial District: Eastern District of Kentucky

Overview: The main institution and an adjacent minimum-security camp were activated in 1992. Minimum-security male inmates from the camp provide services for the main institution. FCI rated: 756; FPC: 512.

Location: 75 miles south of Lexington on Interstate 75 and 20 mi. east of London, Kentucky, on the Daniel Boone Pkwy. Go 3 miles north on State Highway 421, then 1.4 miles off 421 on Fox Hollow Road. Served by Lexington Bluegrass Airport and McGhee Tyson Airport in Knoxville, Tennessee.

FCI Marianna
3625 FCI Road Marianna, Florida 32446
904-526-2313, Fax: 904-482-6837
Federal Correctional Institution, Southeast Region

Accredited

Security Level: Medium/Male; High/Female (adjacent Minimum/Female camp)

Judicial District: Northern District of Florida

Capacity: Rated-805. Adjacent camp: Rated-296.

Overview: Opened in 1988, houses male and female inmates in separate areas. Satellite Camp: Opened in 1988, FPC Marianna houses female minimum-security offenders.

Location: In northern panhandle of Florida, 65 miles west of Tallahassee and 5 miles north of Marianna. Off Highway 167. Marianna is served by Tallahassee Municipal Airport and Greyhound. Commercial airports also operate in Dothan (35 miles northwest of the facility), and in Panama City (54 miles south).

USP Marion
Route 5, P.O. Box 2000, Marion, IL 62959,
618-964-1441, Fax: 618-964-1695
U.S. Penitentiary, North Central Region

Security Level: High/Male (adjacent Minimum/Male camp)

Judicial District: Southern District of Illinois

Capacity: Rated-417. Adjacent camp: Rated-296

Overview: Opened in 1963 to replace the former USP at Alcatraz, USP Marion houses male offenders committed from all parts of the country who have demonstrated need for high security confinement. Typically, offenders have serious records of institutional misconduct, have been involved in violent or escape-related behavior, or have lengthy and complex sentences that indicate they require an unusually high level of security. Average age of inmates is 38, with average sentence of 41.1 years. 56.6 percent have been involved in murder and 91.3 percent have a history of some type of violent behavior. Satellite Camp: Opened in 1971, FPC Marion houses minimum-security short-term offenders and offenders nearing completion of their sentences. Inmates comprise a work force for the support and maintenance of the penitentiary and camp area.   Location: 300 mi. from Chicago and 120 mi. from St. Louis, 9 mi. south of the city of Marion. Off interstate 5 via Highway 148 north, east on Little Grassy Road. Served by the Williamson County Airport.

FPC Maxwell (Montgomery)
Maxwell Air Force Base Montgomery, Alabama 36112
334-293-2100, Fax: 334-293-2274
Federal Prison Camp, Southeast Region

Accredited

Security Level: Minimum/Male

Judicial District: Middle District of Alabama

Capacity: Rated-960

Overview: Opened in 1930, FPC Maxwell is the oldest camp in the Bureau of Prisons. It houses male offenders, primarily from the southeastern U.S. Inmates have no records of serious assaults, no sustained medical or emotional problems, have not been convicted of sexual offense and are generally serving sentences of less than 10 years. Inmates serve as an auxiliary work force, primarily in maintenance and grounds keeping, for Maxwell AFB and Gunter AFB.

Location: On the bank of the Alabama River, at Maxwell Air Force Base. Off Interstates 66 and 85. Montgomery is served by Dannelly Field.

FCI McKean
P.O. Box 5000
(McKean County)
Bradford, PA 16701
814-362-8900, Fax: 814-362-3287
Federal Correctional Institution, Northeast Region

Accredited

Security Level: Medium/Male (adjacent Minimum/Male camp)

Judicial District: Western District of Pennsylvania

Capacity: Rated-784. Adjacent camp: Rated-292.

Overview: Opened in 1989, FCI McKean houses male offenders primarily from the northeastern U.S. Average length of sentence is 98 months. The average age of inmates is 36.1 years. Satellite Camp: Opened in 1989, FPC McKean houses male offenders with an average stay of 24 months.

Location: In a rural section of northwest Pennsylvania on the edge of the Allegheny National Forest between Bradford and Kane, Pennsylvania, 90 miles south of Buffalo, New York. Off Route 59, one quarter mile east of the intersection of State Route 59 and U.S. Route 219, between Interstate 80 and New York State Highway 17. The area is served by the Buffalo International Airport and Bradford Regional Airport.

FCI Memphis
1101 John A. Denie Road, Memphis, Tennessee 38134-7690
901-372-2269, Fax: 901-380-2462
Federal Correctional Institution, South Central Region
Federal Prison Camp, South Central Region

Accredited

Security Level: Medium/Male
Judicial District: Western District of Tennessee
Capacity: Rated-440. Adjacent Camp (Millington) rated 296.
Overview: Opened in 1977, FCI Memphis houses male offenders primarily from the southeastern U.S. There is also a detention unit for pretrial and pre-sentenced Federal detainees.
Location: In the northeast section of Memphis at the intersection of Interstates 40 and 240. Memphis is served by international Airport.

FCI Memphis Satellite Camp (formerly FPC Millington)
6696 Navy Road Millington, Tennessee 38053
901-872-2277, Fax: 901-873-8202
Federal Prison Camp, Middle Atlantic Region
Security Level: Minimum/Male
Judicial District: Western District of Tennessee
Capacity: Rated-296
Overview: Opened in 1990, FPC Millington is located on the largest inland naval base in the world. The camp houses primarily short-term offenders from western Tennessee, eastern Arkansas, and northern Mississippi. It provides 100 inmates daily to the Naval Air Station for janitorial and maintenance services.
Location: On the U.S. Naval Air Station, Memphis, about 20 miles north of Memphis on Route 51. The area is served by Memphis International Airport (30 miles) and Greyhound.

FDC Miami
33 NE 4th St., Miami, FL 33101-9118
305-982-1114; Fax: 305-982-1357
Federal Detention Center replaces function of MDC Miami. Houses pre-trial inmates, male and female. Administrative. All levels of security. Multistory facility opened 1995.
Capacity: 1,214.

FCI Miami
15801 S.W. 137th Avenue Miami, Florida 33177
305-259-2109, Fax: 305-259-2160
Metropolitan Correctional Center, Southeast Region
Accredited
Security Level: Medium/Male
Judicial District: Southern District of Florida
Capacity: Rated-525. Adjacent camp: Rated-261.
Overview: Returned to original mission as FCI as opened in 1976. Satellite Camp: Opened in January 1992.
Location: In the southwest section of Dade County, 30 miles from downtown Miami. Off the Florida Turnpike (Homestead Extension, 152nd St. exit, 2.5 miles to 137th Street, going south). Miami is served by Miami International Airport.

FCI Milan
P.O. Box 9999, Milan, MI 48160
313-439-1511, Fax: 313-439-0949
Federal Correctional Institution, Mid-Atlantic Region
> Accredited
>
> Security Level: Low/Male
>
> Judicial District: Eastern District of Michigan
>
> Capacity: Rated-1,054
>
> Overview: Opened in 1933, FCI Milan houses male offenders whose ages range from 20 to 71 and whose average length of sentence is 10.7 years. There is also a detention unit for pretrial detainees from the Detroit area.
>
> Location: 45 miles south of Detroit and 35 north of Toledo, near the town of Milan. Off U.S. 23 (exit 27). The area is served by Detroit Metro Airport.

FPC Millington (see FCI Memphis Satellite Camp)

FCI Morgantown
Greenbag Rd., P.O. Box 1000, Morgantown, WV 26505
304-296-4416, Fax: 304-284-3613
Federal Correctional Institution, Mid-Atlantic Region
> Accredited
>
> Security Level: Minimum/Male
>
> Judicial District: Northern District of West Virginia
>
> Capacity: Rated-954
>
> Overview: Opened in 1969, FCI Morgantown houses male offenders with substantial program needs (chemical abuse treatment, vocational training, education, or counseling). Designated inmates must be cleared for FCI Morgantown by the Mid-Atlantic Designator.
>
> Location: In the mountainous region of north central West Virginia, on the southern edge of the city of Morgantown. Off State Highway 8.57 (Greenbag Road). The area is served by the Hartsfield Municipal Airport and Greyhound.

FPC Nellis
Nellis Air Force Base, Area II, Las Vegas, Nevada 89191-5000
702-644-5001, Fax: 702-644-7282
Federal Prison Camp, Western Region
> Security Level: Minimum/Male
>
> Capacity: Rated-415
>
> Judicial District: District of Nevada
>
> Overview: Opened in 1990, FPC Nellis houses offenders who do not have records of escape, violence, sexual offenses, or major medical/psychiatric problems. Inmates serve as an auxiliary work force for Nellis AFB.
>
> Location: 15 miles from downtown Las Vegas, on Nellis Air Force Base, Area II. Off Interstate 15. Las Vegas is served by McCarren International Airport.

MCC New York
150 Park Row New York, New York 10007
212-240-9656, Fax: 212-417-7693
Metropolitan Correctional Center, Northeast Region

Accredited

Security Level: Administrative/Male/Female

Judicial District: Southern District of New York

Capacity: Rated-507

Overview: Opened in 1975, MCC New York is a 12-story, high-rise detention facility housing male and female inmates who appear in Federal courts in the Eastern and Southern Districts of New York and the District of New Jersey. The average length of stay is 90-120 days.

Location: In downtown Manhattan adjacent to Foley Square (Federal courthouse), 2 blocks from the base of the Brooklyn Bridge. New York City is served by Laguardia, Kennedy, and Newark International Airports; Amtrak (Pennsylvania Station 34th Street); and Greyhound (42nd St. Port Authority bus station).

FCI Oakdale
P.O. Box 5060, Oakdale, Louisiana 71463
318-335-4070, Fax: 318-335-3936
Federal Correctional Institution, South Central Region

Accredited

Security Level: Medium/Male

Judicial District: Western District of Louisiana

Capacity: Rated-780

Overview: Opened in 1986, FCI Oakdale was the first facility to be operated jointly by the Federal Bureau of Prisons, the Immigration and Naturalization Service, and the Executive Office for Immigration Review. Its original purpose was to house aliens awaiting deportation proceedings. In November 1986, its mission was changed to house Cuban detainees. An inmate riot in November 1987 destroyed much of the facility, which was reconstructed and returned to full operation in January 1989, housing sentenced aliens and regularly sentenced Federal inmates.

Location: In central Louisiana, 35 miles south of Alexandria and 58 miles north of Lake Charles. On State Highway 165, east of Route 165 on Whatley Road. The area is served by Esler Regional Airport (50 miles from the facility), and Trailways (service to Alexandria and Lake Charles).

FDC Oakdale
P.O. Box 5060 Oakdale, Louisiana 71463
318-335-4466, Fax: 318-335-4476
Federal Detention Center, South Central Region

Security Level: Administrative/Male; (Adjacent Minimum Male Camp)

Judicial District: Western District of Louisiana

Capacity: Rated-630. Camp: Rated 118.

Overview: Opened in 1990, FDC Oakdale is operated jointly by the Federal Bureau of Prisons, the Immigration and Naturalization Service, and the Executive Office for Immigration Review; it houses criminal aliens awaiting deportation hearings.

Location: In central Louisiana, 35 miles south of Alexandria and 58 miles north of Lake Charles. On State Highway 165, east of Route 165 on Whatley Road. The area is served by Esler Regional Airport (50 miles from the facility), and Trailways (service to Alexandria and Lake Charles).

FTC Oklahoma City (Federal Transfer Center)
7500 S. MacArthur Blvd., Oklahoma City, OK 73159
405-682-4075; Fax: 405-6804041
Security level: all levels, male and female.
Rated capacity: 1,053
Hub for transfer of Federal prisoners nationally. Separate Facility in center for maximum levels. Served by Will Rogers International Airport.

FCI Otisville
P.O. Box 600, Otisville, New York 10963
914-386-5855, Fax: 914-386-9455
Federal Correctional Institution, Northeast Region
Accredited
Security Level: Administrative/Male
Judicial District: Southern District of New York
Capacity: Rated-648. Adjacent camp-100
Overview: Opened in 1980, FCI Otisville houses an overflow of pretrial and holdover inmates from MCC New York.
Location: In the southeast part of New York State, near the Pennsylvania and New Jersey borders. The institution is 70 miles northwest of New York City, near Middletown. On Route 211. The area is served by several airports, the closest being Stewart International Airport at Newburgh, New York (30 minutes away). Bus and train service connect Otisville to New York City.

FCI Oxford
Box 500, Oxford, WI 53952-0500
608-584-5511, Fax: 608-584-6371
Federal Correctional Institution, North Central Region
Accredited
Security Level: Medium/Male (adjacent Minimum/Male camp)
Judicial District: Western District of Wisconsin
Capacity: Rated-586. Adjacent camp: Rated-156.
Overview: Opened in 1973, FCI Oxford houses male long-term offenders primarily from the north central U.S. Satellite Camp: Opened in 1985, FPC Oxford serves as a satellite facility to the main institution. It houses short-term nonviolent offenders who do not need ongoing care, drug or alcohol treatment, or vocational training.
Location: In rural central Wisconsin, 60 miles north of Madison. Off U.S. 1 (Westfield exit, proceed west on Country Trunk E to County Trunk G, south to the institution). The area is served by Dane County Regional Airport. Greyhound provides service to the nearby towns of Portage and Wisconsin Dells.

FCI Pekin
PO Box 7000, 2600 5. 2nd St. Pekin, IL 61554
309-346-8588; Fax:309-477-4685

Security Level: Medium/male. Adjacent camp-minimum/female
Rated capacity: 752; camp: 256.
Location: In city of Pekin, east of Illinois river, southeast of Peoria,
Illinois. 160 miles southwest of Chicago. Served by Greater Peoria Municipal
Airport. Opened late 1994.

FPC Pensacola
110 Raby Ave., Saufley Field, Pensacola, FL 32509-5127
850-457-1911, Fax: 850-458-7295
Federal Prison Camp, Southeast Region

Accredited
Security Level: Minimum/Male
Judicial District: Northern District of Florida
Capacity: Rated-354
Overview: Opened in 1988, FPC Pensacola houses male offenders primarily from
the southeastern U.S. who do not have records of escape, violence, or major
medical or emotional problems, and have not been convicted of sexual offenses.
Inmates serve as an auxiliary work force, primarily in maintenance, for the Naval
Air Station.
Location: 175 miles west of Tallahassee and 50 miles east of Mobile, Alabama, on
Saufley Field. Off Interstate 10. The area is served by Pensacola Municipal
Airport and Greyhound.

FCI Petersburg
P.O. Box 1000, Petersburg, Virginia 23804-1000
804-733-7881, Fax: 804-863-1510
Federal Correctional Institution, Mid-Atlantic Region

Accredited
Security Level: Medium/Male (adjacent Minimum/Male camp)
Judicial District: Eastern District of Virginia
Capacity: Rated-828. Adjacent camp: Rated-296
Overview: Opened in 1932, FCI Petersburg houses male offenders primarily from
the eastern U.S. Satellite Camp: Opened in 1978, FPC Petersburg is a minimum-
security facility for male offenders, most of whom will be released to the mid-
Atlantic region of the U.S.
Location: 25 miles southeast of Richmond. Off Interstate 95; take Exit 54 (Temple
Avenue/Highway 144), proceed east approximately 3 miles, turn left on River
Road (Highway 725). The area is served by Petersburg Municipal Airport and
Richmond International Airport.

FDC Philadelphia
Adjacent to Federal Court House, 7th and Arch Streets, Philadelphia PA 19106.
Northeast Region

Designed to house pretrial and unsentenced detainees (both male and female)
appearing in Federal Courts in Northeastern Districts. Due on line 2002.

FCI Phoenix
37900 N. 45th Avenue, Dept. 1680, Phoenix, Arizona 85027
602-465-9757, Fax: 602-465-5133

Federal Correctional Institution, Western Region

Security Level: Medium/Male (adjacent Minimum/ Female camp)

Judicial District: District of Arizona

Capacity: Rated-740. Adjacent camp: Rated-272.

Overview: Opened in 1985, FCI Phoenix houses male offenders primarily from the southwestern U.S. A self-contained jail unit houses holdovers and U.S. Marshals Service airlift inmates. A special housing unit is for administrative detention and disciplinary segregation. Satellite Camp: Opened in 1989, FPC Phoenix houses minimum-security female offenders who do not have any significant history of violence or escape.

Location: 10 miles north of the city of Phoenix. Off Interstate 17 (Pioneer Road exit). The area is served by Phoenix Sky Harbor International Airport, 7 regional airports, Greyhound, and Trailways.

FCI Ray Brook
P.O. Box 300, Ray Brook, New York 12977
518-891-5400, Fax: 518-891-0011
Federal Correctional Institution, Northeast Region

Accredited

Security Level: Medium/Male

Judicial District: Northern District of New York

Capacity: Rated-780

Overview: Opened in September 1980, FCI Ray Brook was formerly the Olympic Village for the 1980 Winter Olympic Games. It houses male offenders from the northeastern U.S.

Location: In the Adirondack Mountain region of upstate New York, midway between the villages of Lake Placid and Saranac Lake. Off Route 86. The area is served by the Adirondack Airport (Saranac Lake), Albany Airport (2 hours away), and the Burlington (VT) Airport (2 hours away).

FMC Rochester
P.O. Box 4600, 2110 East Center Street Rochester, Minnesota 55903-4600
507-287-0674, Fax: 507-287-9601

Federal Medical Center, North Central Region

Security Level: Administrative/Male/Female

Judicial District: District of Minnesota.

Capacity: Rated-677

Overview: Opened in 1985, FMC Rochester formerly was a State mental hospital. It serves as a major psychiatric and medical referral center for the Federal Prison System. There is also a work cadre who serve as a manpower resource. The average offender age is 39 years, with a median sentence length of 60 months. A national population is served by the medical staff, although non-patients are primarily from the upper midwest.

Location: In southeastern Minnesota, 2 miles east of downtown Rochester. Off State Highway 296 (Fourth Street). The area is served by Rochester Airport and Greyhound.

FCI Safford
RD 2 Box 820, Safford, Arizona 85546-9729
602-428-6600, Fax: 602-348-1331
Federal Correctional Institution, Western Region

Accredited

Security Level: Low/Male

Judicial District: District of Arizona

Capacity: Rated-421

Overview: Opened in 1964, FCI Safford was originally a minimum-security FPC. Opened as an FCI in 1984; houses male offenders from southwestern U.S.

Location: Southeastern Arizona, 127 mi. northeast of Tucson, 165 mi. east of Phoenix. Off Highway 366, 7 mi. south of town of Safford. Served by Tucson Airport, Phoenix Airport, and Greyhound and Bridgewater Bus to Tucson and Phoenix airports.

MCC San Diego
808 Union Street, San Diego, California 92101-6078
619-232-4311, Fax: 619-595-0390
Metropolitan Correctional Center, Western Region

Accredited

Security Level: Administrative/Male/Female

Judicial District: Southern District of California

Capacity: Rated-612

Overview: Opened in 1974, MCC San Diego was the first of the Bureau of Prisons' high-rise detention facilities, with 12 stories. It houses male and female detainees held primarily for immigration violations, i.e., illegal entry and alien smuggling. The next most common offenses for which pretrial and pre-sentenced offenders are housed are narcotics violations, bank robbery, and probation and parole violations. A sentenced work cadre serves as a manpower resource.

Location: In downtown San Diego, connected to the U.S. Courthouse via a secure tunnel. San Diego is served by Lindberg Field, Amtrak, and Greyhound.

FCI Sandstone
Kittle River Rd., Sandstone, Minnesota 55072
320-245-2262, Fax: 320-245-0385
Federal Correctional Institution, North Central Region

Accredited

Security Level: Low/Male

Judicial District: District of Minnesota

Capacity: Rated-376

Overview: Opened in 1939, FCI Sandstone houses male offenders with an average age of 35.5 years and serving an average sentence of 7.3 years.

Location: 100 miles northeast of Minneapolis/St. Paul and 70 miles southwest of Duluth. Off Interstate 35 (Sandstone exit, follow Highway 23 to Route 123 east). The area is served by Greyhound.

FCI Schuylkill
P.O. Box 700, Minersville, Pennsylvania 17954
717-544-7100, Fax: 717-544-7225
Federal Correctional Institution, Northeast Region

Security Level: Medium/Male (adjacent Minimum/Male camp)

Judicial District: Eastern District of Pennsylvania

Capacity: Rated-729. Adjacent camp: Rated-296.

Overview: Opened in 1991, the institution houses male offenders from the Northeastern U.S. A pretrial detention unit was opened in January 1992. Satellite Camp: Opened in 1991, the camp houses minimum-security male offenders, who provide services for the main institution.

Location: 175 miles north of Washington, D.C., and 46 miles north of Harrisburg, Pennsylvania. One-eighth mile west of Interstate 81. off State Highway 901. The area is served by Harrisburg International Airport.

FCI Seagoville
2113 N. Highway 175, 5eagoville, TX 75159
972-287-2911, Fax: 972-287-5466
Federal Correctional Institution, South Central Region

Accredited

Security Level: Low/Male

Judicial District: Northern District of Texas

Capacity: Rated-977

Overview: FCI Seagoville was originally opened in 1940 to house Federal female offenders. The facility served as a detention facility during World War II for Japanese, German, and Italian families. In 1945, after the war, Seagoville became a Federal Correctional Institution for male offenders. FCI Seagoville houses male offenders from the south central U.S. whose average length of sentence is 9 years.

Location: 11 miles southeast of Dallas, off Highway 175 (Hawn Freeway). The area is served by the Dallas-Fort Worth International Airport.

FDC SeaTac
PO Box 68955, 2425 South 200th St, Seattle WA 98168
206-870-5700; Fax. 206-870-5717
Western Region

Security level: Administrative/Male/Female

Judicial District: Western Washington

Capacity: 677 (When fully activated, SeaTac's capacity will be 677.)

Location: 12 miles south of Seattle, and 16 miles north of Tacoma, 1 mile west of Interstate 5 (200th Street exit). The SeaTac International Airport is 1 mile from the facility. Amtrak and commercial bus lines also serve the area.

FPC Seymour Johnson
Caller Box 8004, Goldsboro, NC 27533-8004
919-735-9711, Fax: 919-735-0169
Federal Prison Camp, Mid-Atlantic Region

Security Level: Minimum/Male

Judicial District: Eastern District of North Carolina

Capacity: Rated-576

Overview: Opened in 1989, FPC Seymour Johnson houses male inmates primarily from the southeastern U.S. who do not have records of escape, violence, sexual offenses, or major medical/psychiatric problems. Inmates serve as an auxiliary work force for Seymour Johnson Air Force Base. The new facility encompassing 60 acres was activated in April 1991.

Location: Near Goldsboro, North Carolina, on Seymour Johnson Air Force Base. Off Interstate highways 40 and 95 and U.S. 70. The area is served by the Raleigh/Durham International Airport (60 miles northeast of the facility), Kinston Airport (26 miles south), and Greyhound.

FCI Sheridan
PO Box 8000, 27072 Ballston Road, Sheridan, Oregon 97378-9601
503-843-4442, Fax: 503-843-3408
Accredited
Security Level: Medium/Male (adjacent Minimum/Male camp)
Judicial District: District of Oregon
Capacity: Rated-923. Adjacent camp: Rated-512.
Overview: Opened in 1989, FCI Sheridan houses male offenders primarily from the Western U.S. Satellite Camp. Opened in 1989, FPC Sheridan serves as a satellite facility to the main institution. It houses minimum-security male offenders.
Location: In northwestern Oregon in the heart of the South Yamhill River Valley, 90 minutes from Portland. Off Highway 18 on Ballston Road. The area is served by Portland International Airport.

MCFP Springfield
P.O. Box 4000, Springfield, Missouri 65808
417-862-7041, Fax: 417-837-1717
Medical Center for Federal Prisoners, North Central Region
Accredited
Security Level: Administrative/Male
Judicial District: Western District of Missouri
Capacity: Rated-912
Overview: Opened in 1933, MCFP Springfield serves as a major medical, surgical and psychiatric referral center for the Federal Prison System and the U.S. Courts. The average inmate is 36 years old. A work cadre serves as a man-power resource.
Location: In Springfield at the corner of Sunshine Street and the Kansas Expressway. Off Interstate 44, Springfield is served by Springfield Municipal Airport, Greyhound, and Trailways.

FCI Talladega
565 East Renfroe Road, Talladega, Alabama 35160
205-362-0410; Fax: 205-315-4495
Federal Correctional Institution, Southeast Region
Accredited
Security Level: Medium/Male (adjacent Minimum/Male camp)
Judicial District: Northern District of Alabama
Capacity: Rated-644. Adjacent camp: Rated-296.

Overview: Opened in 1979, FCI Talladega houses male offenders from the southeastern U.S. Satellite Camp: Opened in 1989, FPC Talladega serves as a satellite facility to the main institution. It houses minimum security male offenders primarily from the southeastern United States.

Location: In the foothills of Northern Alabama, 50 miles east of Birmingham and 100 miles west of Atlanta. Off Interstate 20 on Renfroe Road.

FCI Tallahassee
501 Capital Circle, N.E. Tallahassee, Florida 32301-3572
904-878-2173, Fax: 904-216-1299
Federal Correctional Institution, Southeast Region

Accredited

Security Level: Low/Male

Judicial District: Northern District of Florida

Capacity: Rated-652

Overview: Opened in the late 1930's, FCI Tallahassee houses male offenders primarily from the southeastern U.S. A 308-bed Federal Detention Center, separate from the FCI, is scheduled for activation in Fall 1992 and will house primarily pretrial detainees.

Location: Three miles east of downtown Tallahassee. On Highway 319 at the intersection with Park Avenue. Tallahassee is served by Tallahassee Regional Airport.

FCI Terminal Island
Terminal Island, California 90731
310-831-8961, Fax: 310-732-5335
Federal Correctional Institution, Western Region

Accredited

Security Level: Medium/Male

Judicial District: Central District of California

Capacity: Rated-452

Overview: Opened in 1938, FCI Terminal Island served as a Naval disciplinary barracks from 1942 to 1950 and as a medical facility of the California Department of Corrections for a short time after 1950. In 1955, the institution was reacquired by the Bureau of Prisons. It now houses male offenders and serves as a medical referral facility for the Western Region, providing short-term medical care.

Location: In Los Angeles Harbor between San Pedro and Long Beach. Off Harbor Freeway to San Pedro (cross the Vincent Thomas Bridge and take Seaside Avenue to the Main Gate). The area is served by Los Angeles International Airport and Long Beach Airport.

USP Terre Haute
Highway 63 South, Terre Haute, IN 47808
812-238-1531, Fax: 812-238-9873
U.S. Penitentiary, Mid-Atlantic Region

Accredited

Security Level: High/Male (adjacent Minimum/Male camp)

Judicial District: Southern District of Indiana

Capacity: Rated-741. Adjacent camp: Rated-340.

Overview: Opened in 1940 as the first penitentiary for adult felons to be constructed without a wall, USP Terre Haute houses male offenders with extensive criminal records and who are considered to be sophisticated offenders requiring close supervision. The average inmate is in his early 30's and is serving a sentence of more than 10 years, for either drug law violations or bank robbery. Satellite Camp: Opened in 1960, FPC Terre Haute serves as a satellite facility to the main institution.

Location: Two miles south of the city of Terre Haute, which is 70 miles west of Indianapolis on Interstate 70. On Highway 63. Terre Haute is served by Hulman Regional Airport and Greyhound.

FCI Texarkana
PO Box 1500, Texarkana, Texas 75505
903-838-4587, Fax: 903-223-4424
Federal Correctional Institution, South Central Region

Accredited

Security Level: Medium/Male (adjacent Minimum/Male camp)

Judicial District: Eastern District of Texas

Capacity: Rated-749. Adjacent camp: Rated-220.

Overview: Opened in 1940, FCI Texarkana houses a variety of male offenders, including inmates completing their sentences begun at other institutions. Inmates are primarily from the south central and southeastern U.S. Satellite Camp: Opened in 1981, FPC Texarkana houses a variety of offenders, primarily from the south central and southeastern U.S., including direct court commitments and inmates transferred from other institutions finishing longer terms.

Location: In Northeast Texas near the Arkansas border, 70 miles north of Shreveport, Louisiana, and 175 miles east of Dallas-Fort Worth. Off Route 59 South, on Leopard Drive.

FCI Three Rivers
P.O. Box 4000, Three Rivers, Texas, 78071
512-786-3576, Fax: 512-786-4909
Federal Correctional Institution, South Central Region

Security Level: Medium/Male (adjacent Minimum/Male camp)

Judicial District: Southern District of Texas

Capacity: Rated-784. Adjacent camp: Rated-192.

Overview: Opened in 1990, FCI Three Rivers houses minimum and medium custody offenders from the southwestern United States. Satellite Camp: Opened in 1990, FPC Three Rivers houses 150 minimum-security male offenders, most of whom provide services to the main institution.

Location: The 302-acre site is located about 80 miles south of San Antonio, Texas, and 73 miles northwest of Corpus Christi, Texas, on Interstate 37, and 9 miles west of Three Rivers, Texas, near the Choke Canyon Reservoir.

FCI Tucson
8901 South Wilmot Road Tucson, Arizona 85706
602-574-7100, Fax: 602-670-5674
Federal Correctional Institution, Western Region

Accredited

Security Level: Medium/Male, Administrative/Male/ Female

Judicial District: District of Arizona

Capacity: Rated-389

Overview: Opened in 1982, FCI Tucson houses male offenders, including pre-trial offenders, and those who have been sentenced and await transfer to other Federal facilities. Additionally, a small pretrial and short-term female population is housed at FCI Tucson.

Location: In southern Arizona, 10 miles southeast of the city of Tucson near Interstate 10 and Wilmot Road. Tucson is served by Tucson International Airport, Amtrak, and Greyhound.

Waseca FCI
P.O. Box 1731, Waseca, MN 56093
507-835-8972; Fax. 507-837-4558
North Central Region

Opened June 1996. Male. Low security. Rated capacity 334.

Location: Southern Minnesota. 75 miles south of Minneapolis, off Interstate 35, state highway 14.

FPC Yankton
Box 680, Yankton, South Dakota 57078
605-665-3262, Fax: 605-665-4703
Federal Prison Camp, North Central Region

Security Level: Minimum/Male

Judicial District: District of South Dakota

Capacity: Rated-655

Overview: Opened in 1988, FPC Yankton, a former college, houses male offenders primarily from the Midwestern U.S. who do not have records of escape, violence, sexual offenses, or major medical/psychiatric problems. The average inmate is 36 years old and serving a sentence of 53 months for a drug-related offense.

Location: In the southeastern corner of South Dakota, approximately 60 miles northwest of Sioux City, Iowa, and 85 miles southwest of Sioux Falls, South Dakota. Off U.S. 81 in the town of Yankton. The area is served by airports in Sioux City and Sioux Falls and a municipal airport in Yankton.

FCI Yazoo City
PO Box 5050, Yazoo City MS 39194
601-751-4800; Fax: 601-751-4905
Southeast District

Security Level: Low/Male

Judicial District: Southern Mississippi

Capacity: 1536

Location: About 60 miles north of Jackson, Mississippi, off highway 49. The area is served by most major carriers at the airport in Jackson. Yazoo City also is served by Amtrak and commercial bus lines.

APPENDIX C

Federal Bureau of Prisons: Corrections and Detention Division

Called the Community Corrections Centers by the Prison Bureaus of each state and the federal government, halfway houses are the final destination for the majority of inmates nearing the end of their prison sentences.

They are better known as halfway houses because when you get there, you are halfway home and still halfway in prison.

Most inmates are eligible for halfway house time, except "maxing out" or "going to the gate" prisoners. Infractions they committed in prison has cost them their "good time" off and halfway house eligibility.

Halfway houses are designed to provide prisoners with a sense of security. Believe it or not, many who have spent time in a structured environment do welcome some continued order under which to operate once they leave the prison...for a little time anyway.

Rules at halfway houses are similar to those of most institutions, though the accommodations may not be as sanitary as they were in prison.

Half way houses are supervised by Community Correction Management Centers. Your family or friends will be directing their requests for information from these centers as your halfway house date nears.

It is also the director of each who decides whether or not your halfway time will be honored as figured out by your case worker.

If his shelters are tight for bed space, you may find yourself spending an additional week or two longer in the prison than you thought you would have to spend. It may help to have a nagging family member ring him up daily asking for a status report.

Community Corrections Management Offices

ATLANTA CCM OFFICE
505 McDonough Blvd. SE
Atlanta, GA 30315
404-624-8141, Fax: 404-624-8145
Districts: Northern Florida, Northern/
Middle/Southern Georgia/South
Carolina

BALTIMORE-MARO CCM OFFICE
10010 Junction Drive, Suite 101-N
Annapolis Junction, MD 20701
301-317-3280, Fax: 301-317-3138
Districts: Maryland, Delaware, District
of Columbia, Northern Virginia, West
Virginia, Eastern Virginia

BOSTON CCM OFFICE
JFK Federal Bldg.-Suite 2200
Boston, MA 02203
617-565-4293, Fax: 617-565-4297
Districts: Massachusetts, Vermont,
Connecticut, Maine, Rhode Island,
New Hampshire

CHICAGO CCM OFFICE
200 W. Adams, Suite 2915
Chicago, IL 60606
312-886-2114, Fax: 312-886-2118
Districts: Central/Northern Illinois/
Eastern/Western Wisconsin

CINCINNATI CCM OFFICE
36 East 7th Street, Suite 2107-A
Cincinnati, OH 45202
513-684-2603, Fax: 513-684-2590
Districts: Eastern Kentucky, Southern
Indiana, Northern/Southern Ohio

DALLAS CCM OFFICE
207 South Houston St., Room 144
Dallas, TX 75202
214-655-5050, Fax: 214-655-5060
Districts: Oklahoma, Northern Texas

DENVER CCM OFFICE
1961 Stout Street, Rm. 683
Denver, CO 80294
303-844-5176, Fax: 303-844-6189
District: Colorado

DETROIT CCM OFFICE
1850 Federal Bldg., Detroit, Ml 48226
313-226-6186,Fax: 313-226-7327
Districts: Michigan, Northern Indiana

EL PASO CCM OFFICE
208 Mesa One Building
4849 North Mesa St.
El Paso, TX 79912
915-534-6326, Fax: 915-534-6432
Districts: New Mexico, Western Texas
(Midland, Pecos, Del Rio, and El Paso
Division)

HOUSTON CCM OFFICE
515 Rusk St., Rm. 12016
Houston, TX 77002
713-718-2781, Fax: 713-718-4780
Districts: Southern/Eastern Texas

KANSAS CITY CCM OFFICE
U.S. Federal Courthouse
500 State Avenue, Rm. 237
Kansas City, KS 66101
913-551-5714, Fax: 913-551-5718
Districts: Northern/Southern Iowa,
Kansas, Nebraska, Western Missouri

LONG BEACH CCM OFFICE
501 West Ocean Boulevard, Suite 3260
Long Beach, CA 90802-4221
310-980-3536, Fax: 310-980-3543
District: Central California

MIAMI CCM OFFICE
401 North Miami Avenue
Miami, FL 33128-1830
305-536-5705; Fax: 305-536-6530
Districts: Puerto Rico, Virgin Islands,
Southern Florida

MINNEAPOLIS/ST. PAUL CCM
Federal Office Building
212 3rd Ave., S., Rm. 135
Minneapolis, MN 55401
612-334-4073, Fax: 612-334-4077
Districts: North Dakota, South Dakota,
Minnesota

MONTGOMERY CCM OFFICE
P.O. Box 171,15 Lee Street
U.S. Courthouse, Rm. B-18
Montgomery, AL 36101
205-223-7480, Fax: 205-223-7012
Districts: Southern/Middle/Northern
Alabama, Southern/Northern Missis-
sippi, Northern Florida

NASHVILLE CCM OFFICE
U.S. Courthouse, Rm. 599
Nashville, TN 37203
615-736-5148, Fax: 615-736 5147
Districts: Eastern/Western/Middle
Tennessee, Western Kentucky

NEW ORLEANS CCM OFFICE
701 Loyola Ave., Rm. T-3034
New Orleans, LA 70113
504-589-6646, Fax: 504-589-2378
Districts: Louisiana, Arkansas

NEW YORK CCM OFFICE
26 Federal Plaza, Rm. 36-110
New York, NY 10278
212-264-9520; Fax: 212-264-9516
Districts: Southern New York, New Jersey

ORLANDO CCM OFFICE
135 W. Central Blvd., Suite 650
Orlando, FL 32801
407-648-6055, Fax: 407-648-6058
District: Middle Florida

PHILADELPHIA CCM OFFICE
1880 John F. Kennedy Blvd., Suite 602
Philadelphia, PA 19103
215-587-1582, Fax: 215-656-2050
Districts: Eastern/Middle Pennsylvania

PHOENIX CCM OFFICE
234 N. Central Ave.-Suite 425
Phoenix, AZ 85004-2212
602-379-4947, Fax: 602-379-4061
Districts Southern California, Arizona

PITTSBURGH CCM OFFICE
411 7th Avenue, Room 1204
Pittsburgh, PA 15219
412-644-6560, Fax: 412-644-3408
Districts: Northern/Western New York,
Western Pennsylvania

RALEIGH CCM OFFICE
310 New Bern Avenue, Rm. 325
Raleigh, NC 27611-7743
919-856-4548, Fax: 919-856-4777
Districts: Southern West Virginia,
Eastern/Middle/Western North Carolina,
Western Virginia

SACRAMENTO CCM OFFICE
3522 Federal Building
650 Capitol Mall, Room 3522
Sacramento, CA 95814
916-498-5718, Fax: 916-498-5723 ·

District: Eastern California

SALT LAKE CITY CCM OFFICE

US. Courthouse, 350 S. Main Street,
Rm. 503
Salt Lake City, UT 84101
801-524-4212, Fax: 801-524-3112

Districts: Utah, Wyoming, Nevada,
Idaho

SAN ANTONIO CCM OFFICE
727 E. Durango-Room 138
San Antonio, TX 78206
210-472-6225, Fax: 210-472-6224
District: Western Texas

SAN FRANCISCO CCM OFFICE
450 Golden Gate Ave., Rm. 145458
P.O. Box 36137
San Francisco, CA 94102
415-436-7990, Fax: 415-436-7995
Districts: Northern California, Guam,
Hawaii

SEATTLE CCM OFFICE
160 Jackson Federal Bldg.
915 Second Ave.
Seattle, WA 98174
Districts: Alaska, Oregon, Western/
Eastern Washington, Montana

ST. LOUIS CCM OFFICE
Federal Court House
1114 Market St.-Room 902
St. Louis, MO 63101
314-539-2376, Fax: 314-539-2465
Districts: Southern Illinois,   Eastern
Missouri

APPENDIX D
STATE DEPARTMENTS
OF CORRECTIONS

If you need information about someone in a State prison you can search "The Corrections Connection" on the Web or, better yet, call the phone number provided below for your State's Department of Corrections.

Alabama Department of Corrections: 334-240-9501

Alaska Department of Corrections: 907-269-7400

Arizona Department of Corrections: 602-542-5536

Arkansas Department of Correction: 501-247-6200

California Department of Corrections: 916-445-7688

Colorado Department of Corrections: 719-579-9580

Connecticut Department of Correction: 860-566-4457

Delaware Department of Correction: 302-739-5601

District of Columbia Department of Corrections: 202-673-7316

Florida Department of Corrections: 850-488-5021

Georgia Department of Corrections: 404-656-4593

Hawaii Department of Public Safety: 808-587-1288

Idaho Department of Correction: 208-334-2318

Illinois Department of Corrections: 217-522-2666

Indiana Department of Correction: 317-232-5715

Iowa Department of Corrections: 515-281-4811

Kansas Department of Corrections: 913-296-3310

Kentucky Department of Corrections: 502-564-4726

Louisiana Department of Public Safety and Corrections: 504-342-6741

Maine Department of Corrections: 207-287-4360

Maryland Department of Public Safety and Correctional Services: 410-764-4003

Massachusetts Executive Office of Public Safety: 617-727-7775

Michigan Department of Corrections: 517-373-0720

Minnesota Department of Corrections: 612-642-0200

Mississippi Department of Corrections: 601-359-5621

Missouri Department of Corrections: 314-751-2389

Montana Department of Corrections: 406-444-3930

Nebraska Department of Correctional Services: 402-471-2654

Nevada Department of Prisons: 702-887-3285

New Hampshire Department of Corrections: 603-271-5600

New Jersey Department of Corrections: 609-292-9860

New Mexico Corrections Department: 505-827-8709

New York Department of Correctional Services: 518-457-8126

North Carolina Department of Correction: 919-733-4926

North Dakota Department of Corrections and Rehabilitation: 701-328-6390

Ohio Department of Rehabilitation and Correction: 614-752-1164

Oklahoma Department of Corrections: 405-425-2500

Oregon Department of Corrections: 503-945-0920

Pennsylvania Department of Corrections: 717-975-4860

Rhode Island Department of Corrections: 401-464-2611

South Carolina Department of Corrections: 803-896-8555

South Dakota Department of Corrections: 605-773-3478

Tennessee Department of Correction: 615-741-2071

Texas Department of Criminal Justice: 409-294-2101

Utah Department of Corrections: 801-265-5500

Vermont Department of Corrections: 802-241-2442

Virginia Department of Corrections: 804-674-3000

Washington Department of Corrections: 360-753-1573

West Virginia Department of Military Affairs and Public Safety: 304-558-2037

Wisconsin Department of Corrections: 608-266-4548

Wyoming Department of Corrections: 307-777-7405

About the Author

Jim Tayoun has peppered his six plus decades in this life with three 2 year terms in the Pennsylvania State House of Representatives, four 4-year terms in the Philadelphia City Council, 19 years as a newspaperman, while sandwiching all the above with his role as manager of his family's famed Middle East Restaurant in the historic district of Philadelphia. He considers his prison time as his fourth career change, and looks to further writing as his fifth.

Acknowledgments

Special thanks to Marlyn and Norman Kline for their enthusiasm as they turned my loose sheets of notes into almost a fait accompli through their desktop publishing skills and for shepherding the various editions since; to former inmates Arnold Biegen, for bringing his New York presence as a learned and capable attorney to our nightly conferences in the prison library; to inmate Arnold Packer, for his New Hampshire penchant for double checking all the facts to insure accuracy and for his overview of our goals; and Riccardo J. Suarez of Palm Beach for corroborating the testimony of other inmates from penitentiaries down through his own experiences; to the Food Service Foremen at Schuylkill Prison Camp, who didn't mind having to track me down to the library when I wasn't at my desk; to the Schuylkill Prison Camp staff for their encouragement and suggestions as well as to all the inmates who gave me the benefit of their years of experience in confinement in all levels of the Federal prison system; and to my wife, Dolores, who willingly and encouragingly worked her copying machine overtime.

ORDER FORM

Please send

_____ copies of *Going to Prison?*
at $9.95 each .... _____

Sales tax, Maine sales only,
5.5% .... _____

Shipping, add $2.00 for first book,
$.50 each additional book.
(Add $4.00 for priority shipping.) .... _____

Total .... _____

Send check or money order payable to:
Biddle Publishing Company
PMB 103
P.O. Box 1305
Brunswick, Maine 04011

Name _____

Address _____

_____

Phone _____